A DOSE OF REALITY

E.R. SILVERBUSH

First edition
Copyright © 2024 by E.R. Silverbush
All rights reserved

Cover art by Mickey Chan

No portion of this book may be reproduced in any form without written permission from the author, except as permitted by U.S. copyright law.

The events in this book are portrayed to the best of the author's memory. While the stories are true, some names and identifying details have been changed to protect privacy. In very few cases, events have been compressed for brevity and clarity.

The conversations come from the author's recollection and are likely not word-for-word transcripts. However, at the very least, the essence of the dialogue is accurate.

This book contains copyrighted song lyrics, the use of which have not been specifically authorized by the copyright owners. However, they are used within the fair use doctrine of US copyright law.

To Sandy, for putting up with me.
And for Maya, Talia, and Pepper. I really hope you never read this.

As I stumbled through Manhattan's Herald Square, mumbling to myself like a typical homeless New Yorker, families and other tourists stopped, stared, and got out of my way. But a glimpse of my reflection in a hotel window forced me to pause. The image of my scraggly hair, unkept beard, and skinny torso made me cognizant of my fate in life. If only I could remember how I ended up here.

The historic Hotel Pennsylvania was steps from the city's most famous attractions. Directly across from Madison Square Garden, the enormous complex was in a perfect location. That is, if you were part of the herds visiting the Empire State Building and, this time of year, Rockefeller Center. Times Square was up the road, and while New Year's Eve mayhem was only a day away, most visitors would avoid the area for now. After all, this was 1994. The city had not yet undergone its extraordinary transformation from grit to glitter. The era was pre-Giuliani, pre-Bloomberg, and pre-Sarah Jessica Parker.

The lobby's quintessential NYC energy was amplified by glimmering decorations and cheer. For someone on the cold, hard sidewalk, it looked warm and aspirational. It would be a shame to ruin that holiday spirit, but I was hungry and confused, and there was only one way to get help. Nervously pacing back and forth, I contemplated the magnitude of what was about to happen. At seventeen, I'd already become like the cardboard box bums I'd see when my family visited the city. But I mustered the courage to go inside, hoping my actions would help turn it all around.

Entering through the revolving doors, my body thawed, and I absorbed the lobby's pulsating energy. The air smelled like mulling spices, and *Jingle Bells* put a pep in everyone's step. There were couples, yuppies, and children who had come to the world's greatest city for a glimpse of everything it had to offer. They were about to get more than they bargained for.

It's doubtful anyone took note of me in my dirty Lollapalooza T-shirt and torn jeans. But as I methodically undressed, that changed. First came the shoes and socks, and then my shirt. Clumsily, I removed my pants. Stumbling through the lobby, nearly tripping over myself, I placed my tighty-whities on the marble tile. There I stood, butt-ass naked, in the middle of a meticulously decorated holiday scene in one of Manhattan's most highly-trafficked hotels—like the ultimate ornament on an X-rated Christmas tree.

ONE TO GROW ON

"You fucked him?" a busty fifteen-year-old Trina asked her slightly younger friend Karrie Christensen, who smiled through crooked teeth and a Marlboro Red.

"BJ," she replied, shaking her head. "He didn't have a rubber."

As I sat on my new 1984 teal Predator bike outside Fay's Drugstore, I tried to figure out what these girls were talking about. But my best friend, Darren, followed along perfectly. After all, I was six; he was nine. We tried all winter to beat *Super Mario Brothers* on my Nintendo, and all of a sudden, it was April. The snow was melting, and the annual freeze that consumed the city for six months each year had started to subside. If the sun was out, we couldn't stay in.

Darren lived a few doors down from me, and we'd been friends our entire lives. But now our age gap felt wider. We rode here because these girls *he* knew wanted Wacky Fruit Bubble Yum and cigarettes. As they stubbed out their butts to go inside, I dropped my bike and followed. "Watch this," Darren said, as newly installed automatic doors opened and closed with his movements. I hadn't seen anything like that before.

As I tried to figure out how the doors knew when to move—I was pretty sure magic wasn't real—a young girl, blonde and petite, walked towards us holding her father's hand. It was my crush, Jill Campbell. I had never seen her outside school before.

As her dad gave us a disapproving look, I blurted out, "Hi, Jill." But they blew right past me like I didn't even exist.

"Who's that?" asked Trina.

"My girlfriend." That drew some chuckles and a "Yeah right," so I left it at that, and we ventured into the store.

My mom dragged me to Fay's all the time, and I had the trip down to a science. On the way in, I'd check the payphone for quarters and take note of what goodies were in the capsule machines. Then, while my mom shopped or talked some random customer's ears off, I'd pick something from the toy aisle—a cap gun or water balloons—to take home. But while that was fun for *me*, I couldn't understand why these big kids were so excited to be here. When we bypassed the toys for the pharmacy section, I grew even more confused—especially when Trina picked up a box of something called Trojans that, judging by the color of their boxes, came in two flavors: cherry and blue raspberry.

Next up was the music aisle, where I noticed Trina wasn't holding the Trojans anymore. When she shoved a Bangles tape down her pants and Darren motioned for me to be quiet, I understood what was happening. In the blink of an eye, we were almost through the exit when a voice called my name. A tall seventeen-year-old with gold studs in his ear towered over me. It was Jimmy Ellis, a guy from my street who treated me like a little brother. He was clearly suspicious, but when I said we were just getting candy, he believed me. After giving him a high five, the older kids and I walked out scot-free—but not before I checked the capsule machines for any left behind quarters.

After Fay's, Darren and I rode to his house, passing through various parts of our neighborhood, nicknamed "The Westcott Nation" after the eponymous street on which we lived. An eclectic place, its old Victorian homes were inhabited by Syracuse University students and young professors, along with hipsters, single-parent households, and a few working-class families like my own. On the way, we passed a pizza place, an ice cream shop, a new age bookstore, a minimart, a liquor store, and a movie theater that had recently made the switch from pornos to second run films. We got to Darren's and immediately turned on my Nintendo—he often borrowed mine—and got to work.

"Today is the day, I can feel it!" he said, beginning a game of *Super Mario Brothers*. His mom, Tina, was a single and free-spirited biker chic. She stood in front of a full-length mirror, brushing the long, blonde hair that almost reached her tall, leather boots.

"Hey E.R. play me a song, would ya?" Tina said, referring to a dusty, out of tune upright piano near the window overlooking the porch. Like a lot of parents in the neighborhood, she got a kick out of watching me play, as if they'd never seen someone do it in real life. Usually I would oblige, but didn't she understand we were on our way to beating King Bowser? I looked to Darren for guidance, but he had pretended not to hear.

"I know you can pause that thing," she insisted.

We tried explaining our superstition that if you paused a Nintendo for too long, it would reset. But Tina's darting glance said we had no choice. So I sat at the bench and played a Chopin Nocturne, the soft melody contrasting sharply with the *High Times*, *Tattoo Magazine*, and *Fabulous Freak Brothers* issues on the nearby coffee table. While I liked the attention of moments like these, I hated taking lessons and practicing. Not that I had any say in the matter.

My dad taught me piano every Sunday, just like he had done for my siblings. I also had to play for twenty minutes each day. It was the only form of structure or discipline I had other than having to show up at Hebrew School, go to Synagogue on the High Holidays, and attend an occasional concert at the Syracuse Symphony.

"Are you kidding me?!" Darren yelled, cutting through the Chopin and jolting my attention back to the TV. The Nintendo flickered between the start menu and a bunch of garbled images. It had, indeed, reset. As we blew on the cartridge to remove any dust, Tina finished getting ready and left us alone to hit up the bars down the street.

* * *

By 8 p.m., Darren and I had given up on Mario Brothers and were watching *Friday the 13th* when a group of college students wheeled a keg into the house next door. Darren gave me a little nudge with his elbow to look out the window. "A keg," he said. "They're going to tap it."

Darren once told me he helped his mom "tap the keg" when she had friends over in the summer. I didn't know what that meant, but I imagined a bunch of tattooed guys in leather vests gently tapping a barrel with their fingers to prevent it from exploding, like I did with my bottles of Coke. But I had it all wrong. The students stuck a pole into the metal barrel, filling cups for a small crowd that appeared out of nowhere.

"Come on," Darren said, walking towards his back door. "Let's go."

"I have to be home by nine," I informed Darren, although he already knew that.

"It's like 8:30. You got a ton of time."

When we arrived at the neighbors' backyard, I expected curious, disappointing looks and a stern warning to go home. And when some guy pouring a beer spotted us, it looked like that was going to happen.

I thought, *We're in trouble*, until his face lit up with a smile and he yelled, "Entertainment's here!" They were more than happy to have us over, and before long, two guys in bent-brimmed white hats—that ubiquitous frat boy accessory—held Darren up as he did a keg stand. The crowd cheered him on.

"Six! Seven! Eig—"

Darren signaled to be put down. As he stood up with a semi-wobbly smirk on his face, someone yelled, "Eight seconds!" which reminded me I needed to get home.

"Excuse me, mister, what time is it?" I asked the first person I saw, who seemed to give the question more consideration than it warranted.

"It's Miller time!" he screamed and headed over to the keg.

* * *

"Do you know what time it is?" my dad, Abe, asked. His thick Eastern European accent complimented his protruding Eastern European belly. As I walked up to the porch, he was more concerned than angry.

"Nine?" I asked, hopeful.

"It's 10:30. Get inside."

My mother, CeCe, sat at the dining room table when I entered, which meant something was up. I glanced over her shoulder at the living room, where the NBC Special Presentation logo appeared on the Zenith TV. I was hoping for *This is Your Life*. My parents loved watching famous people get stunned in front of a studio audience while dramatic music played. But it was a news piece on the maiden voyage of the Space Shuttle Challenger. My dad walked to the TV and turned it off. He had five words for me. "Jimmy Ellis came by today." Uh oh.

Jimmy told them I was stealing and smoking, which I vehemently denied. Technically, the latter was true, but I kept that to myself. Although for my mom, the most pressuring issue concerned the girls. "Is she Jewish?" It was a ridiculous question, not only because I was six, but because there weren't any other Jewish kids for miles. To placate her, I said yes, the girls were Jewish. But she couldn't leave it at that—she needed proof. So she asked for her last name, and I told her the truth: Christensen.

My mother laughed off my foolishness but proceeded to grill me on the terrible report card I'd received a couple weeks back. I was promising the next one would be better when my dad interrupted. But his concern wasn't about school; he never cared much about that.

"I don't want you running around with those kids," he said. "They're bad news."

"They're my friends. And they're *not* bad news." That was a lie; they were pretty bad. But who else was there to play with? Yet, as my dad spoke, it was clear I'd no longer be allowed to hang out with the older kids. And although my parents had virtually zero influence on my day-to-day activities, I sort of agreed.

I stood up to go upstairs when my dad interrupted. "Did you practice piano today?"

* * *

Even though I was in trouble, I went to bed smiling. Visions of summer filled my brain — mischief and discovery were around the corner. But when I woke, the air felt different. Cold. I looked out my window to see my lawn covered in inches of snow, with more falling. *Damnit*, I thought. A surprise storm on the weekend. One last snow day would have been awesome.

Normally on a day like today I'd go to Darren's to cut through his backyard and sled down the vacant lot above his house. But after last night, there was no way that was happening. And anyway, a young professor had purchased the home next to the lot and planted bushes to prevent any sledding. While it was still ten years before McDonald's infamous "hot coffee" lawsuit, America was becoming a highly litigious place.

As I came downstairs for Saturday morning cartoons, my mom called out, "Do you know someone with the last name Gillard?" Her head was buried in *The Syracuse Post Standard*. "Eighteen years old," she continued. "He was caught doing marijuana." CeCe liked to read the police blotter to see if anyone I hung out with had been arrested. It was seriously annoying.

"Mom," I said, in a tone suggesting of course I didn't know this person. But that didn't satisfy her, so I said finally said no.

"Well, if you do, stay away from them."

Ignoring this routine of ours, I poured a bowl of cereal. My huge dog, Chewbacca—a neighborhood menace—came over anticipating scraps. My dad had spent part of his youth as a shepherd in Siberia and had a real love for herding dogs. Dressed in his usual JCPenney short-sleeve button-down shirt and brown polyester pants, he put down the national news section and chimed in.

"Marijuana? Those damn hippie kids ruined this country." He turned to me. "Stay away from them."

"I don't know him," I reiterated.

He took one last sip of coffee. "Come on, Junior, let's go."

"Where?"

"Sledding." He smiled.

"Yes!" I let out. What a surprise.

My dad's big, red Chevy van was as much of a neighborhood staple as our dog. The "Silverbush Upholstery" stenciled in big, cursive letters left no doubt in the mind as to who was in that vehicle. As one might imagine, it didn't make me very popular at school. It also took forever to heat up. As I sat there bundled up, steam escaped my mouth with every breath.

After a few minutes of driving, my dad noticed I was shivering. "When I was your age," he began, "I spent two days in a wagon in weather that would make this look like Hawaii." As we made our way across the heavily salted streets, he appeared lost in thought before continuing the story. "There was this one kid who thought his toes were going to freeze off, so he peed in his boots to warm them up. But then the pee froze." He laughed as if reminiscing about an old prank phone call. As he continued to drive, I thought about last night and my report card.

"Dad, did you do good in school when you were a kid?"

His initial chuckle was disarming but quickly turned into a more serious facial expression. He was lost in thought and not saying ... anything. He looked old and worn, and not without good reason. Most of my friends' parents were barely thirty. He was fifty-five. As I waited for a reply, the wrinkles around his eyes became intense, turning from solemn to angry.

"Dad?" I said, reminding him of my presence. He snapped back to it, looking at me and forcing a smile before parking. We had arrived at our destination.

I'd never actually been inside Drumlins Country Club, but its hillside eighteenth hole was legendary for sledding. For the occasion, my dad broke out his 1950s-era seven-man toboggan. The huge wooden contraption probably weighed fifty pounds. It was a relic of the past and a fun one at that. As Abe schlepped both me and that toboggan up the hill, a young employee came out and flagged us down.

"I'm sorry, sir, you can't sled here," he respectfully informed us. My dad looked confused.

"It's not allowed. You know, lawsuits and all that."

"I've been coming here for thirty years," he replied, his Eastern European accent becoming stronger. "I took all my kids here."

"Like I said, I'm sorry."

My dad stood there, searching for a way to respond. His survival of both the Holocaust and a Russian gulag had made him resistant to authority. He looked up at the top of the hill and then back down at this twenty-something punk trying to tell him what he can and cannot do.

"Alright. Fine," he said, as we continued up the hill. "We'll just go down once."

The employee quickly ran up in front of my dad, blocking our way. "I'm sorry, I can't allow that."

My dad's entire posture shifted. He was done with the formalities.

"Okay, listen, we're going up the hill. We'll go down once, and we'll leave. That's it, and that's all."

As we climbed to the top, the employee didn't move. If we wanted to sled down this hill, we would have to go through him. Abe didn't have a problem with that. As we stood at the top, there was a moment between the two adults. A dare, perhaps.

"I'd move if I were you," my dad explained. The guy didn't budge, and Abe shrugged, dropped the toboggan, and motioned for me to get in. Seconds later we sped down the hill with increasing velocity, and I fully expected this guy to get the hell out of the way. My dad probably did too.

He didn't.

In a matter of seconds, we barreled over the employee, tipping over our sled. The two men got in each other's face, and Abe didn't waste any time. He picked up the toboggan, held it above his head, and slammed it into the dude's nose. But my father was a man of his word. As the poor guy stood there, bloody and in disbelief, we packed up our things after a single run, got in the van, and headed back home.

* * *

A couple of days after the toboggan incident, I was back at school. While Westcott Street was a potpourri of cultures, Edward Smith Elementary took it up a level with half of its students hailing from nearby housing projects. There, I managed to carve out a niche for myself as a teacher's nemesis. Stealing condoms and going to keggers may have been out of my league, but things here were much more my speed. And by the middle of first grade, most teachers were sure I'd end up a nothing—or worse.

On this particular day, however, I wasn't the one instigating. That honor belonged to Robbie Cornbloom, a slightly chubby kid and my good friend. Robbie lived five blocks from me in a neighborhood more family-oriented, with two spouse households and not a college student in sight. He was the only person I knew with a computer—a Commodore 64—and the only friend I had my age. The kids on Westcott were all either older or younger.

Robbie had brought a ripped-out page from the Sears Christmas catalog that was making its way around the classroom. But this wasn't torn from the toys section; there were no transformers or G.I. Joes here. Instead, an attractive and very busty woman was showcasing a new bra. As she made her way from desk to desk, Miss Fishman, our red-headed teacher a few years out of grad school, wrote on the blackboard.

Our class had great timing. Every time Miss Fishman turned to face us, the photo was out of sight and everyone kept a straight face. But I was lost in a daydream about Jill Campbell, who sat in the first row. So, when the bra pic was tossed my way, bypassing the empty seat next to me to land on my lap, I was startled. Jason and Jared, two clean-cut popular kids, laughed like they actually wanted me to get caught. I quickly snatched up the paper.

Staring at the gigantic gazongas, I struggled not to laugh. As the boy next to me, Henry Gillard, motioned to pass it over, I cupped my mouth. But that only made a fart-like noise that caused a bunch of kids to giggle and Miss Fishman to whip around. But everything looked perfectly in order. Too much in order. Miss Fishman sensed something was up but went back to writing math problems on the board.

"Yo, give it here," Henry pleaded. That's when I remembered I *did* know a Gillard. That must have been Henry's big brother who was in the police blotter. I tried to slyly hand the paper over, but I dropped it, and we bumped heads trying to pick it up.

"Ouch," I let out as Miss Fishman turned around. She walked straight to my desk, looming over me and my balled-up hand.

I tried playing dumb, but Fishman meant business, so I reluctantly opened my palm, and the wad of paper tumbled to the ground. When she uncrumpled it, her face conveyed about half a second of sheer shock before she calmly explained that Principal Howard might stop by the classroom today—part of her monthly rounds—so it was crucial for us to be on our best behavior. She gave us a writing exercise to fill the time as she tidied up for the potential visit.

Instead of participating in the assignment, I pulled a container of Elmer's Glue from my desk, planning to spread it over my hands and revel in the sensation of peeling it off. But then I saw the unmistakable green and white dot matrix booklet on the corner of Miss Fishman's desk. It was the annual school contact sheet. Its storied pages contained the addresses and phone numbers of every student at Ed Smith. Even Jill Campbell's. I couldn't believe Miss Fishman had left it there.

While Fishman cleaned up, I put the glue down on the empty seat next to me, inadvertently leaving the cap off, and quietly walked to her desk to grab the book. As I made my way back, however, the classroom door opened, and Miss Howard appeared. With all eyes focused on her, I went to my desk and dropped the phone sheets inside. As Mrs. Howard paced around the classroom, examining with the sternness and authority of Darth Vader, Miss Fishman looked worried. Ultimately, as anyone could have predicted, the principal's eyes landed upon me. Then Fishman looked *very* worried.

"How's your desk, E.R.?" asked Mrs. Howard. "Cleaner than last time, I hope?"

Just the other day, Miss Fishman had made me stay after school to clean my notoriously messy desk, nudged by an appalled Mrs. Howard. So she was confident that its current state of organization would impress. Little did she know that the phone book was in there. As Howard made her way to the empty seat next to me, I had no choice but to open it. But, as our much-feared principal sat down, she immediately stood up and let out a loud, piercing shriek—her soaking wet butt the unmistakable bright white color of having sat in a full bottle of Elmer's Glue.

* * *

The mustard-yellow telephone was strategically placed between our kitchen and living rooms, making it accessible from many areas of the house—as long as the cord stretched that far. But on this Sunday evening, that location couldn't have been worse. Before hiding the class list under my bedroom dresser, I wrote down Jill's number and worked up the courage to call her. The problem was that the people sitting around the table inadvertently prevented me from speaking to the love of my life.

My parents and two of my brothers, Mark and Jeff, were having what might be considered a family meeting, and the agenda was me. I eavesdropped while waiting for a good chance to grab the phone and take it into the basement stairs for privacy. My mom was visibly nervous, biting her nails while her eyes fixated on something in her mind. I had seen this look before.

CeCe, like her own mother, had severe anxiety issues that at times bordered on illness. She would often run things over and over in her head, or out loud, hoping that if she did that enough times, reality would bend in her favor.

"I'm not letting them hold him back, and he's *not* being tested," she proclaimed to my dad, who was busy reading the paper. *Tested?* I wondered. Tested for what?

My brothers, meanwhile, were turned towards the living room where *The Wiz,* the all-black TV adaptation of the *Wizard of OZ,* played. I loved that movie. Michael Jackson was my idol. My twelve-year-old sister, B'nai, couldn't have agreed more.

"Maybe he *is* retarded," Mark joked, while Jeff—wearing a Miami Dolphins hat—hit him to say, "That's not funny." Was I going to take some sort of special ed test?

"So, go talk to them like you always do," my dad told CeCe while keeping his eyes on the paper.

"Oh, I'm going to," she affirmed, thinking for a moment before continuing, "I don't understand; they all say he's smart. If he's so smart, who cares about his math score? Send him to second grade, he'll pick it up there. That's what happened last year."

"Did he pick it up?" Mark asked sarcastically. It was no secret that I'd struggled with math all year long. But it was also reading. And science. And history. Heck, even gym. I had received nearly all N's—non-satisfactory—on my report card all year. And while the bar at Ed Smith was set very low, I was unable to even meet those standards. As a result, Mrs. Howard suggested I get tested for special needs. The alternative was an ultimatum: One more screw-up, and I'd have to do first grade all over again.

My mom turned to my brothers for advice. Typically, parents wouldn't ask a six-year-old's siblings to weigh in on such life-altering decisions, but as the youngest of six—these two knuckleheads were already twenty and twenty-two years old—it made sense. My oldest brother, Brad, was a married lawyer in suburban New York City, so he wasn't around to offer his opinion. But any of them had more insight into a child of the 80s than my parents. My mom married Abe in 1955, right out of high school. And my dad's childhood activities included preventing his mother and siblings from starving to death.

While the family discussed the unlikely case that I'd be able to finish the year without another behavioral catastrophe, I snuck by and grabbed the phone. The cord stretched just enough to get me through the basement door, which I quietly closed behind me while using my index finger to slowly dial. I had played this scene out dozens of times in my head, and in every single case, Jill picked up the phone. But I was sure that the older, masculine voice who impatiently said "hello" wasn't her.

"Is Jill home?" I asked. There was a long pause on the phone before finally, "Who's this?"

After explaining that I went to school with Jill, Mr. Campbell sternly informed me she wasn't available. Then I got nothing but the unmistakable "screw you" sound of dial tone. I was dumbfounded. I furiously picked the phone up and called again but got the same response. So, I called a third time, and no one picked up. And then a fourth time, and a fifth time, until I gave up.

I cracked the basement door to get a glimpse of my family. My mother had made up her mind—as if there was any question to begin with. She would give both my teacher and principal a piece of her mind. There was no way I was being tested, and no one was holding me back. Case closed.

The next day, the school week began as normal with the trading of scratch and sniff stickers until the bell rang, and Miss Fishman ushered us into our seats. But this Monday was different.

"Good morning, everyone. Before we start sharing time, I wanted to tell everyone that it is not acceptable to call your classmates outside of class, unless, of course, it's okay with both the person and his or her parents."

What? Jill's dad called the school on me? Well, at least Ms. Fishman had the decency not to call me out by name. Or so I thought, until she turned to me and said, "E.R., Jill's parents would very much appreciate it if you would stop calling her." I looked over at Jill, who had her head down, mortified.

YOU CAN LEARN A LOT FROM A DUMMY

Over the next few years, I rarely saw Darren. He dropped out of school and, like most older kids in the neighborhood, got involved in things I knew little about. But my parents' hopes that I'd get my act together were sorely misguided. And while my mom called Principal Howard's bluff—I passed first grade—my second-grade teacher also wanted to hold me back. As did my third. And my fourth, fifth, six, and so on. But each year, CeCe successfully argued my way to the next grade. And now, in 1992, I was a fourteen-year-old high school freshman at William Nottingham High School.

"What's crack?" my mom asked as I grabbed a box of Apple Jacks from the cupboard. The answer wasn't a problem; it was the question that perplexed me. "Jaru Williams was arrested for it on the south side," she said, trying to trick me into admitting I knew a crack dealer. "Mom, stop," I uttered, eating my breakfast before heading to the O'Conner's house. I'd been friends with five of the seven Irish Catholic siblings since birth, but it was only recently that eleven-year-old Timmy and I had become inseparable.

The frenetic energy at the O'Conner's was a stark contrast to my house. Seven kids ranging from six to thirty scrambled to get ready for their day. As I waited for Timmy, his sixteen-year-old sister, Pam, passed by with barely so much as a hello. You never knew what you were going to get with her. Had she been in a friendly mood, I might get a peek at a boob or maybe even her vagina. Today? Nothing.

After a long day of roaming the neighborhood, me, Timmy and his five-year-old brother, Finn, engaged in one of our favorite pastimes: trying to hit cars, trucks, or buses with rocks, snowballs, or golf balls. But we hadn't had any luck, and it was getting dark. I was thinking of going home when we saw the oncoming headlights of Ziggy's Wagon—a precursor to the food truck—a guy who drove around the university selling late night munchies to drunk and stoned college kids. I'd never met Ziggy or been on campus late enough to buy anything from him. But I'd seen the van, and now that it was coming up Westcott, it was go-time.

I grabbed a rock from the ground and imagined I was Dan Marino—I'd been a Dolphins fan ever since my brother Jeff rooted for them in Superbowl XVII. My throw was timed perfectly, hitting the truck right between the numbers, AKA the windshield. I basked in glory for about two seconds before things went awry. Unlike most vehicles we hit, Ziggy stopped, got out, and chased us. But he had no chance. We knew the backyards and fences behind every house in a one-mile radius.

These types of pursuits happened a lot, and we had a specific yet unspoken protocol. If one of us runs, we all run. We didn't look back or ask questions, and we always separated to make it harder to find us. And after jumping over a couple of backyard fences and crossing a road, I was in the clear a few blocks away. I was sure the others were fine too, but I didn't want to return to the scene of the crime or risk going home to find the cops there. So I took off my shirt, making it harder to identify me, and walked calmly to Robbie Cornbloom's house.

Robbie had been the one consistent friend in my life, and when I wasn't hanging around Westcott with the O'Conners, I was at his place watching the R-rated movies my parents would never allow. My plan was to call home to see if the police were there and then leave if the coast was clear. But when my dad picked up and told me to get there right away, I knew it was bad. Turned out not all of us got away from Ziggy. Five-year-old Finn got caught, and he sang like a bird.

Thankfully, Ziggy had gone to high school with one of my brothers, so he was going to let the whole thing slide. No authorities involved.

* * *

April 29th began like any other day of freshman year—with me not going to class. The problem was that I had nowhere to go, so I typically hung around the hallways or on school grounds. Today, I was huddled in a second-floor hallway with five of my black classmates— Peanut, Pooh, Meatball, Clayton, and TJ— rolling dice with a messy stack of dollar bills next to us.

The game was Cee-lo, which I'd just learned how to play. As I took my turn, the guys were arguing about which Public Enemy song was better, "911's a Joke" or "Can't Truss It." I was a big fan of the former, but I kept my mouth shut and rolled the dice. As is so often the case with beginners, I had a streak of luck. No one was happy when I won the thirty-five-dollar pot.

"Don't give that white boy my money," Clayton said, snatching the cash out of my hand. He had been released from Juvie a couple weeks ago and ended up at Ham, so we didn't know each other, and I had no clue how this would play out. But the other guys intervened, explaining I was cool. Because Nottingham put its low achievers in the same classes together, I'd gotten to know these guys pretty well, often taking the bus together to the all-you-can-eat buffet at Ponderosa or to play *Street Fighter* at an arcade. After some reluctance, Clayton handed my money back.

Nottingham was always a shit show, but it was getting even worse. And there was little that our principal, Dr. Mayo, was willing—or able—to do about it. Skipping school was as easy as walking out the door, and as I headed towards the main entrance thirty-five dollars richer, a ruckus behind me suggested that the Cee-lo crew had changed their forgiving minds. But when I saw a small crowd parading around a white mannequin with a noose around its neck, it was obvious this had nothing to do with me. The Rodney King cops had just been acquitted.

Somehow, in a way that would only make sense at Nottingham, what began as a demonstration against racial injustice spiraled into a black vs. Puerto Rican melee—with both girls and guys involved. Punches were thrown, weaves went flying, and the crowd picked up steam as it moved into the main lobby and towards the front doors. By the time Dr. Mayo and our school cop, officer Sanders, arrived on the scene, the situation was far out of control. Yet, the sight of the universally loathed Mayo served as the catalyst for a kumbaya moment, in which, for one split second, the students united as one. In the blink of an eye, someone picked up an industrial-sized garbage can and nailed Mayo in the head with it, knocking him over to jubilant cheers.

Over the following months, Nottingham became even more unruly. On most mornings, my dad would drop me off at the main entrance and I'd walk straight out the back door. But now that it was the middle of winter, it was a real problem not to have anywhere to go. My house wasn't an option because my dad came home for lunch. Eventually, I started using the spare key hidden in Robbie's mailbox to hang out there.

It was a perfect set up, and no one — including Robbie — had any idea. Over a few hours, I would play video games and watch movies until I could go home. Today I planned to do exactly that, only this time the key didn't seem to be there. I was digging into the mailbox, feeling around with my fingers, when a car slowed down as it passed. I acted like I was supposed to be there, confidently searching for the key, and let out a sigh of relief when the vehicle passed without stopping.

My plan B was the O'Conner's. I could get in through a basement window under their porch. No one would be home, but I rang their doorbell to double check. Then I knocked, rang another time, and knocked again. The coast was obviously clear, so I climbed through the window and went to the living room to play Madden football.

As I powered up the Sega Genesis, a voice called out, "What the fuck?!" It was Pam. Why wasn't she in school? Why didn't she come to the door when I rang the bell? I nervously tried to explain that I was there to pick up a game I left behind before she screamed, "Get the fuck out of here before I call the police." She didn't have to tell me twice.

I had no choice but to go back to Nottingham, using the pay phone to check in with my dad—maybe Pam actually called the cops. He was furious. Pam hadn't called the police, but she did tell her parents, who called the school, who notified my dad. But that wasn't the worst of it. The people who drove by Robbie's house were his neighbors. They were keeping an eye on the place because Robbie's parents suspected someone had been breaking in. It turned out I didn't clean up well enough after making some of their Velveeta mac & cheese, and apparently wearing an aqua and orange Dolphins windbreaker in the heart of Bills country was a dead giveaway.

Robbie's father called my dad for an explanation, and in a matter of hours, I lost all my friends. Robbie and I were still cool, but I wasn't allowed over. Meanwhile, the entire O'Conner family had shunned me.

When school was out, I flew out to Los Angeles with my parents and B'nai to see my sister Penny. She got married when I was around three, moved there, and before long made me a six year-old uncle. Each summer we would visit, and every time I'd fantasize about going to a high school that looked like 90210's West Beverly. Without that trip, the summer of 1992 would have been a lonely one. I was hoping sophomore year would be better, even if I was repeating most of the same classes.

* * *

In September, I quickly found out two things: Pam had been home that day because she was pregnant, and Nottingham had a new principal. Our fearless leader was Gabriel Williamson, a relatively young professional who had already made a name for himself for being tough and effective. He arrived at 'Ham ready to make serious changes, like a zero tolerance policy on violence that led to the prompt expulsion of many of the school's most dangerous students. But the most drastic measure he took, the one that actually impacted *my* day-to-day, was creating a network of gym teachers and administrators who spent much of their day roaming the halls with walkie-talkies. Nottingham became a bootstrapped, high-school version of Big Brother. Skipping was now impossible.

My one respite from torturous classrooms was lunch in the cafeteria. With no group of friends to call my own, I moved from table to table until I ended up at the same spot each day with classmates I knew from different contexts. There were Jonah and Elias from Hebrew school—together we were three of the five Jews in our class of over two hundred. Joe, a chubby kid, was hiding an issue of *Hustler* behind a textbook. Ryan was a straight cut guy who already had his driver's license, and he was good friends with Omar, the one black dude at our table. While our school was over fifty percent black, he had the distinction of being the only one who looked like Kurt Cobain. Next to him was Klaus, a Lacrosse-playing giant; a hipster named Derek Castle; and Shayan, an Iranian-American I was constantly arguing with about such important matters as which girls were most attractive or which one of us loved hot wings the most.

With the exception of Joe, who lived in a real rough area, these guys were from a part of town that bordered on suburbia—yards away from being in the Jamesville Dewitt school district, AKA JD, which served some of the county's most affluent families. Many kids in my Hebrew school went there.

"Why are you studying?" I asked Jonah. "It's *lunch.*" "Because it's the SATs," he responded dryly, like I was an idiot.

I had to ask for clarification because I had never heard of the SATs, a fact that shocked everyone. Will, a skinny kid with Brandon Walsh-inspired sideburns, overheard this as he sat down. He was the only other person at school who watched 90210—*Martin* and *Family Matters* were far more popular. He asked, "What do you want to be when you grow up?"

I'd only recently given that any thought. After the whole thing with Timmy and Robbie, I'd been spending a lot of time at home watching cable TV, which my parents had just gotten after years of begging. One of my favorite channels was E!, which gave fascinating insight into the Hollywood film industry. I somehow worked up the fantasy of attending USC or UCLA to become a movie producer. It didn't at all sound like a pipe dream to me, at least not until these guys said I'd *definitely* need to take the SATs to get into *any* school, let alone one of that caliber. Little did they know I would have been lucky enough to graduate with C's and D's.

"I'll probably just go to OCC."

"COMMUNITY COLLEGE???!!!" they nearly said in unison, as if that was the craziest thing ever.

All of my siblings—except for Jeff, who went to SU for music—attended local Onondaga Community College, not because they couldn't get in elsewhere, but because it was their only financially viable option. Yet all were successful, white-collar professionals, so I knew that I could always turn it around there.

Despite the gaps in our upbringing and neighborhoods, the lunch table guys and I became friends, eventually calling ourselves "The Crew" or "The Crizzew" in gangster rap dialect. So, during a massive snowstorm on New Years' Eve 1993, I left a Zima and buddha-fueled party at Darren's—my first time hanging with him in two years—and trekked for an hour in my Dolphins Starter to Elias' house. That was where the rest of The Crew was hanging, along with a nerdy Hebrew School dude named Eric who Elias was friends with. My presence didn't exactly sit well with the parents, and when El's dad, a doctor, opened the door, he was suspicious.

It may have only been in my head, but it felt like he was mentally frisking me for drugs or alcohol. It was insulting, but I couldn't blame him for imagining such things given the circumstances. Once inside, I was directed to Elias' room in the basement, where the guys were playing *Magic: The Gathering*. I pulled a couple bottles of Zima from my jacket and tossed them on the bed.

"Your dad should have searched me," I said. "There's more buried out front in the snow."

I was the only one of us who had ever been stoned or drunk, and everyone was furious that I'd suggest something as insane as drinking alcohol on New Year's Eve. But the night was emblematic of my overall relationship with these guys. I adamantly believed that enjoying life and working hard in school were mutually exclusive, and that this was not the time to be focused on the latter. I grew up around siblings who reminisced about their good old days, so I had a visceral sense of the fleeting nature of youth, and I would not squander that by sitting in a classroom. It was a strong point of contention between us, but tonight was a lost cause. I was wondering what I was going to do with the unused booze when all of a sudden Hebrew school Eric opened a Zima and chugged it. It would be just he and I drinking to ring in 1994.

* * *

Each Sunday, my parents went to Wegmans, the highly respected cultural icon of Central New York. It was a place where the rich, poor, black, and white went grocery shopping—a consumerist metaphor for how the world should be. There I would read Entertainment Weekly and film industry magazines, one day coming across an article on an unknown independent film called *Dazed and Confused*. The Crew had zero interest in seeing a movie about a bunch of burnouts, but I managed to convince them. The film made drinking and smoking look sexy and fun, and it had an effect on them. As soon as it was over, they asked me to score some weed.

The next weekend I showed up to Elias' basement with some pot I'd picked up from a Westcott connection and 40's of *Crazy Horse* from a corner store that didn't ID neighborhood kids. Before long, we were fucked up in that ridiculously stupid teenage kind of way. While Elias' parents were out to dinner and a movie, he was banging away on his piano. Joe, for his part, was bench pressing fifty pounds with the intense look of an Olympic competitor. Jonah was freaking out about cleaning up before El's parents came home, while Will, Klaus, Derek, and Omar were pontificating on how Rage Against the Machine's issue-driven music was going to change the world. Then we saw that Shayan was missing.

Those of us coherent enough to care searched the house and eventually found Shai in the kitchen, walking around with his pants around his ankles. Thankfully, he still had his boxers on.

"It's big D time!" he yelled enthusiastically, before shouting, "Shear beer bear!"

Shear beer bear was our euphemism for sex, or something we'd say to each other whenever we saw a cute girl at the mall. Of course, none of us were actually shear beer bearing, so we inevitably needed a word for making out, which for one reason or another became chicka frown down.

We yelled at Shai to pull up his pants—most of us with our eyes closed. Ultimately, he calmed down, and we all went back to the basement together. But a moment or so later, Shai proclaimed he needed to tell his mom how happy he was. Several of us tried to subdue him from picking up the phone, but he got a hold of it and dialed. While we tried to pry the device out of his hands, his mom picked up, and we had no choice but to let the man talk.

"Salam, Mom?"

Shai's parents had come to the United States after the Iranian Revolution, and they had high expectations for him.

"What time are you gonna' pick me up?"

Shai spoke in a mishmash of English and Farsi, all the while alternating between the running-man dance and shadow boxing while explaining the situation to his mom. "I feel like dancing."

A pause, while we all wondered, *WTF?*

"'Cause I drank some orange juice earlier, and … it's so weird."

At that moment, Shai slapped his hand on his forehead, realizing how ridiculous this sounded, and promptly hung up on his mother. That's when we called it a night.

*　*　*

While I had been rubbing off on The Crew, getting them to let loose and booze it up, the life lessons weren't exactly reciprocal. While they were buckled down on academics, I was screwing up worse than ever. Nevertheless, my parents were happy about the new crowd I was running with, especially now that I had a couple of Jewish friends. They took this as an opportunity to sign me up for a regional Jewish Youth convention, called USY, in Albany. And while I could have gotten out of it if I wanted to, their level of seriousness indicated it wouldn't be worth the trouble. Instead,

I convinced Elias to come with me, and we brought along a bag of weed.

Elias and I spent most of the first day in Albany finding people who would be down to smoke and trying to devise a plan to get away with it. The activities we had to attend were even more boring than school—prayer classes, Israeli history, and the like. But there was one session that stood out. There was concern in the American Jewish community that its teens were getting brainwashed by cults, sometimes never to be heard from again. So, our guest speaker was a professional deprogrammer who helped such families bring their kids back to reality. His gripping talk of subliminal messaging and mind control techniques was possibly the first time I ever paid attention in something resembling a class.

After a Shabbat dinner, a DJ played Van Morrison's "Brown Eyed Girl," and everyone rushed to the dance floor. I didn't know the song and couldn't understand why everyone was so excited. But I recognized it was the perfect opportunity for me, Elias, and three new friends to sneak out the side door and huddle in a patch of grass running alongside the building.

It was a warm night for May, and quiet enough that our every sound reverberated, increasing the chances we'd get busted. As Elias, along with a hippie girl named Rachel and two different Joshes, stood around waiting, I took an old, crinkled sandwich bag out of my pants and pulled out an eighth of weed, a small metallic bowl, and a mini Bic lighter. A few moments later, and the five of us were getting ripped. Our efforts at silence were thwarted every time someone hacked up a lung.

As we passed the bowl and shared common stories and experiences, the Jewish-American culture I knew so little about opened before my eyes. It was surprising to find I had so many things in common with people I had nothing in common with. It was like an inside culture that I had unintentionally been left out of. That's when Rachel asked if I like Phish—a very unusual question.

"Not really. I mean, salmon is okay." Everyone except me and Elias laughed at this joke that wasn't actually a joke.

"Wait, did you actually think I meant fish, like, that you eat? Did you?"

My silence said it all, and as the unmistakable laughter of stoned teenagers filled the warm spring air, the side door snapped open, and a counselor appeared. I jammed the bowl in my pocket, and before she knew what to make of the situation, we went inside. As Billy Joel's "Piano Man"—another song foreign to me—blared, these kids sang along jubilantly to every single damn word.

*　*　*

For over a decade, frustrated teachers had declared to me, "You won't be laughing in June." It was a warning that while I took school as a joke, there would be a reckoning come spring. They were always right. It was now the last day of junior year, and I had failed several classes. If I wanted any shot of graduating, I had to take Spanish over in summer school. But I still had a week or two to fret about that. In the meantime, I wanted to kick the summer off right, popping a tab of LSD and preparing to trip for the first time.

During the last day of the USY convention, the words Phish and LSD had been brought up a dozen times. I'd become determined to try the latter, so I reached out to my old friend Darren, who hooked it up. I then rummaged around my brother's old room to find something psychedelic to bring along with me, coming across his old *Dark Side of the Moon* double record set. I had never listened to the album but had read about it. When I opened up the cover, a folded-up poster, part of the set, fell out. It didn't look like much except a large field of grass with the great pyramids of Egypt in the background. I brought it along with me.

By noon, I was sitting on Elias' kitchen floor staring at the poster. The grass morphed into ghoulish faces that swirled in front of my very eyes. I had been in that position for half an hour while the rest of The Crew drank beer and took a dip in Elias' pool. When I eventually snapped back to it, I went for a walk in the backyard, which had a small stream running through it. I took in the sounds of nature while contemplating the meaning of life, the trivial nature of happiness, and other thoughts that were sophomoric and cliched but novel to me. It was like seeing the world as it really was for the very first time in my life.

This Zen-like state was abruptly shattered when Ryan—the only one of us who didn't smoke and barely drank—approached me wearing one of Elias' old Halloween masks, fucking with me. It was freaking me out, but telling him to knock it off only egged him on. To show I was serious, I went inside, grabbed a kitchen knife, and threatened him. A couple of the guys tried to intervene, and after a brief struggle, I came to my senses, dropped the weapon, and ran upstairs to once again be alone with my new thoughts. But as I opened a bedroom door, I was greeted by Shayan's ass in the air—he was banging his girlfriend, Tammy. Without so much as a glance behind him, he kicked the door closed again.

Tammy lived a couple blocks off Westcott with her mother and three siblings. Her younger brother, Rich, had been in and out of juvie twice by thirteen. Her mother, Deena, was single and loved to smoke pot with the neighborhood kids. The two youngest girls were regularly exposed to drama, like when Tammy's friend ran over to their house after getting in a fight with her boyfriend, who came looking for her and punched their glass door, shattering it all over himself and earning a police-mandated ambulance ride. None of The Crew guys knew her, but a couple weeks prior, I invited her out for a night out in a playful effort to make Shai jealous that I knew an actual girl. But by the end of the night, she was his girlfriend—whether he liked it or not.

I smoked a stog out back to calm down. The peak of my trip was ending, and while the experience illustrated how quickly a trip could go south, I was enamored with it. I had taken away something meaningful and was dying to do it all over again.

THIS IS YOUR BRAIN ON DRUGS

Westcott Street's *Seven Rays* was a New Age bookstore filled with incense, crystals, and meditation guides. But it was the counterculture section and its books like *PIHKAL: A Chemical Love Story*—a one-thousand-page tome on psychedelics—that piqued my interest. It was a couple weeks after that trip in Elias' backyard, and my new favorite hobby was coming here to sit on the floor and read about drugs, along with actually doing them.

I had decided to let my hair grow long, much to my dad's dismay, which stood in sharp contrast to the tacky Dolphins Starter jacket I still wore. I was playing drums in a "band" with Elias and Omar, using an old kit Mark had left behind when he moved to college years ago, and I'd become obsessed with the sixties, reading about people like Ken Kesey and the legendary acid tests.

One concept that stood out, associated with a man I read about named Timothy Leary, was "ego death." During this part of the psychedelic experience, a person is spiritually reborn through complete transcendence, pure awareness, and ecstatic freedom. That sounded fucking awesome. And while it seemed crazy that Richard Nixon once called Leary the most dangerous person in America, I was sure that my dad, who'd been lamenting hippies since their inception, had agreed with him. But I admired the spirit of that young generation, the courage with which they engaged in drug use, and the societal change they fostered during those turbulent times.

The most striking part of the era to me was 1967's summer of love, and I wanted to have a similar experience over the next couple of months. The challenge was that my summer school had a firm policy: If you miss more than three days total, you automatically fail. And in my case, failing would officially eliminate any possibility of graduating next year. So, those three allowed absences would be used judiciously: one for my first ever Phish show, a second for Lollapalooza, and the third for the twenty-fifth anniversary of Woodstock, which was being held less than a three-hour drive from Syracuse. I was intrigued by the historic event and convinced I would find the spirit of the 60's alive and well there. My parents made it clear there was no way I was going.

Permission was only one obstacle to the festival of a lifetime: I didn't know anyone who could give me a ride, let alone afford the one hundred and seventy five dollars ticket. But when there's a will, there's a way. I spread the word that I had two tickets to the event (not true); and that if someone gave me a ride, they'd get a free ticket (obviously also not true); and I vowed to wear Abe and CeCe down over the next few weeks. I had all summer.

When my parents and B'nai drove to NYC for a World Cup match at Giants Stadium with my brothers, I convinced them to let me stay home. After all, *someone* had to watch our new dog, Cholo, who, like Chewy, was rabidly territorial. But the truth was I wanted to stay because I'd picked up two ten-strips of Felix the Cat acid from a local skater kid named Benji. I invited a bunch of people over, hooked my brother's old stereo speakers up to our TV, and put *Jurassic Park* in the VCR.

After a few hours of acid-induced mayhem, the dozen or so kids trickled out of my house, and it was just me, Shai, and Elias left. We walked to a place known as "Xavier's House," an old, dilapidated Victorian home with chipped blue paint that was faded by years of Syracuse weather and neglect. It was rented, or squatted, by three of the area's most unscrupulous nineteen-year-olds. There was Dave Polish, who went by "Polish," a jacked dude dumb as a rock; Kendall, a tall black kid who had a heart of gold but was equally adept at violence; and Xavier himself, a hot-headed light-skinned dude who was known to go from laughing with you to punching you in the face at the flip of a dime.

The violent trio dropped out of high school years ago yet still maintained close ties to the Nottingham community. So much so that their place became a revolving door of teenagers looking to score, screw, or crash. We slowly entered the pitch-black living room, spun out of our minds, barely able to see two feet in front of us. A rapidly pulsating strobe light suggested vague silhouettes and the jarringly robotic movement of bodies. As "Insane in the Brain" by Cypress Hill blared throughout the house, a voice called out to us.

"If you pussies are here for the math Olympics, they were yesterday." It was Polish, who looked directly at Shayan.

"What's up, Shooshan," he said, botching the name. Shai sheepishly corrected him. "It's Shayan."

"I know your name," he responded. "Keg's upstairs, Shaboo-boo."

When Polish disappeared, the strobe light briefly illuminated a dude blacked-out on the couch. Kneeling on the floor next to him was a man of gigantic proportions, who I optimistically thought was performing CPR. Then I saw a taser gun in his hand. As teenagers who had recently begun getting intoxicated, we knew the typical hijinx—drawing on passed-out friends or putting shaving cream on their hands while ticking their face. But tasing?

That was a new one. And it was scaring the shit out of us.

Buzzzzzzzz!

The sound of this guy getting electrocuted made our jaws drop. One of us gasped a bit too loudly, and the fat man snapped his neck around. The strobe light illuminated his face. He was a dark-skinned Latino, much older than us, whose gold teeth reflected that strobe right back into our eyes. This was Johnny Sabs, and we had heard all about him. An obese, dangerous criminal with a deep, hoarse voice and a long rap sheet, Johnny was probably the last person in Central New York you'd want to be on the wrong side of.

We didn't know much about Johnny's personal life other than he supplied most of our drug dealers and that he once was an assistant coach on the Nottingham football team. He looked at us with a surprisingly welcoming smile, turned back to the guy still passed out on the couch, and continued to tase him. That's when we turned around and walked right out the door.

Stepping out onto the porch was like escaping an asylum. The sounds of birds chirping in the damp, student-less SU-area air seemed tranquil and idyllic. But that was interrupted by an all too familiar bass line thumping in the distance, getting closer by the second. The song was the Fugees' "Killing Him Softly," and it meant only one thing: Tammy. This was her jam—or villainous leitmotiv, depending on context—and she played it on repeat in the busted-up Dodge convertible that she paraded around town like a Ferrari.

Shai and Tammy's relationship was like a Jerry Springer production of a Shakesphere play. They fought. They fucked. They fucked and they fought. Tammy kept tabs on Shayan's whereabouts twenty-four-seven, and when she tracked us down a few moments later—there really weren't that many places to look—the star-crossed lovers screamed at each other, and I almost wanted to go back into the asylum.

* * *

Two weeks after the Westcott Acid Test, Elias drove me, Will, and Derek to a Phish show at SPAC, Saratoga's performing arts center. Despite all the hoopla at USY, I wasn't particularly excited to see the band. It was more about the party and the prospect of finding good acid. It was also a chance for Elias to meet up with an old summer camp friend, Jason Goldstein from Commack, Long Island. We all met up briefly in the parking lot before the show. Jason brought along his friend Craig, who fit the suburban hippie stereotype to a T.

His tie-dyed shirt seemed to play off his lazy eye, together conveying a sense of aloofness and disarray. He and I briefly took part in something I learned was called a drum circle and then separated before going into the show.

SPAC was revered for its expansive lawn, and I imagined the show would consist of peaceful, quiet fans spread out on picnic blankets, smoking pot, and listening intently to the music. And that's pretty much what it was—until the band came on. From that moment, everyone was on their feet, packed like sardines, staring at the musicians on stage, especially the lead guitarist, Trey, who mesmerized everyone with his long, stuffy hair and sorcerer-like playing. In mere minutes, the sounds, smells, and movements of the audience induced sensory overload, and I moved to the back of the lawn to get some space. There were people doing what might generously be described as dancing, and while this noodling looked ridiculous, it was infectious. And by the second set, when the sun set and the acid hit hard, I joined in.

I was starting to understand what this was all about. The music was enveloping me, like I had been wearing ear plugs my entire life. It was a moment of revelation until a girl with a red bandana began yelling "Pez" over and over, killing the mood. This chick really wanted some of the classic candy.

"What??" I turned to her and yelled, annoyed.

"Um … I don't know. What?"

"Why do you keep saying my name?"

"I'm not. I'm yelling 'Pez.'"

"Yeah, that's me."

"Your name is Pez?"

"Uh, yeah."

"That ... is ... so ... cool!!!!!!" she said, hugging me before disappearing into the crowd. I turned my focus back to the music. It was a tune I knew—"Bouncing Around the Room." As I danced, I felt weightless. The song's closing instrumental section, with its lullaby-like piano and soothing guitar, made me feel free. I looked around at others who were in a similar state and sensed a kinship with them. I wasn't exactly sure what was happening, but I knew I wanted to feel this way again.

Towards the end of the show, I was wandering around during a spacey jam and stumbled into an area where dozens of people in zombie-like fazes twirled to the music with a deep void in their dark eyes and a stench of body odor in the air. As I navigated through the musk, their arms were extended and eyes wide open, reminding me of when B'nai and I would watch Michael Jackson's *Thriller* over and over again at a display table at Kmart.

The acid was playing all sorts of spatial and aural tricks on me, and as I picked up the pace to get the hell out of there, someone grabbed me. I turned around, frightened at first, but relieved when I saw it was only Elias, his buddy Jason, and Craig, whose lazy eye seemed to be moving in impossible directions like those red and blue Martians from Sesame Street. Their presence grounded me, but as we spoke, someone wrapped their arms around me like a long-lost friend. It was the girl in the red bandana.

"Pez!!!!"

* * *

One week before Woodstock, someone bit on my generous, albeit fake, ticket-for-ride offer. I'd never met Julien, but he went to school with Colin Murphy, a kid who had lived in my neighborhood until his father finished medical school at SU. His dad, like so many before him, got his family the hell out of Westcott as soon as he could afford to.

My plan was to leave that Friday morning right after my dad dropped me off at school, and I didn't pack anything because it would be an obvious giveaway. So, I brought nothing except the shorts, T-shirt, and sandals I was wearing, and a five dollar bill a classmate gave me to bring him back a hit of acid—Syracuse was completely dry. I should have prepared better, but my excitement to experience the magical sixties era clouded everything.

The one part I did give some thought to was actually getting into the festival. It was a long shot, but I told Julien that I had ordered tickets with my parents' credit card, and they were being held at the will call office. When we got there, I would say the same thing to the people working at will call and pray they showed some sympathy. Hopefully, there was a will call.

Another concern was getting home. I had used my second allowed absence from summer school on Lollapalooza. Not that I had any regrets. Smashing Pumpkins did an incredible job headlining after Nirvana pulled out, shortly before Cobain's suicide. But, if I didn't make it to school on Monday, it would be impossible to graduate next June.

After a three-hour drive, we followed signs to a series of immense parking lots, where festival goers parked before boarding one of the dozens of school buses heading to the concert grounds.

The process was straightforward: a staff member collected your ticket, and another put a bracelet on you before allowing you to board the bus.

"I don't see a will call," I said to Julien. It was a ridiculous thing to say in the middle of vast farmland.

"I'm still not sure how there would be a will call," he responded. "It's not like this is an actual theater."

I hate these smart-ass private school kids, I thought, before deciding we should go through the line to see what happened. The staff members were doing their jobs so haphazardly that when Julien and I passed through, they slapped bracelets on us without even a glance for tickets. A second or two later, we were on the bus, and I was overcome with relief.

At the festival site, it was immediately clear that the entire Woodstock operation fell apart before it even began. Everywhere I looked, fences were being clipped and thousands of ticketless fans were pouring in. Shortly after Julien set up a tent, we got separated. At night, the temperature fell dramatically, and after several hours of searching, I successfully found Julien's empty tent. As I tried to fall asleep, I heard the sound of crickets, Nine Inch Nails performing in the distance, and a woman getting banged by a guy apparently named Ben. Then came the unmistakable thumping of pouring rain.

I woke in the morning to a shit show. The several thousand-acre farm was now a virtual swamp. Hundreds of thousands of cold, muddy, and stoned revelers were ready to not only make the best of the shitty situation, but to relish in it. It was chaotic, it was loud, and it was fun. But it was also stupid. I had been expecting to find the spirit of the sixties here, but all I saw was an over-commercialized shit show—peace, love, and Pepsi. I thought back to that Phish show and how it embodied the genuine hippie way of life more than this place.

I was freezing, and my soaking wet clothes weren't helping. One of the temporary bathrooms had hand dryers, so I sat underneath one for half an hour, which provided short bursts of relief but wasn't actually drying anything. I contorted my body under the device in a desperate effort, but it was a lost cause. As yet another twenty-second cycle ended, some dude walked by with a cup of beer in his teeth. While zipping up his jeans, he used his free hand to hit the start button. As another blast of hot air hit me, he enthusiastically yelled, "Right on, bro!"

There were some bright spots. The band Live, unknown at the time, blew everyone away. Green Day instigated a 50,000-plus person mud fight. But by Sunday, it was obvious I needed to find a ride home, and out of desperation, I left the area hoping to hitch a ride towards Syracuse. There was just one problem: No one was leaving. To the contrary, there was a line of cars miles long—a record-breaking, national-news-making-length line—to get in. My chances of graduating were slim.

After many hours, I made my way out to a jam-packed highway, eventually arriving at a local fire department, where I used the phone to call my parents. They were relieved to hear my voice and said they'd be there in three hours. When they arrived, six hours later, they grounded me for the rest of summer. But that was a symbolic gesture because in a week, school would be over, and I'd be in Los Angeles visiting my sister and nephews. And, indeed, I ended up passing Spanish, which meant it was still possible to graduate—if I somehow pulled off the best academic performance of my life in the fall.

* * *

My time in LA that summer was going to be different, and better, because my parents weren't coming. I was a free man, flush with two hundred dollars to go back-to-school shopping on Melrose Ave. I was also on the hunt for LSD because Syracuse was still dry, and if I brought some back, it would be a huge win. Unfortunately, there was none to be found on the legendary shopping strip, but I did splurge on a T-shirt that read "D.A.R.E. to Keep Cops Off Donuts."

Melrose aside, I spent nearly all of my time in the valley, mostly at the Sherman Oaks Galleria. Usually nothing more eventful than a Hot Dog on a Stick happened, but on this day, I saw a group of kids in the arcade playing *Mortal Kombat* who looked, well, like the west coast version of me: long hair, Chuck Taylor All Stars, flannel shirts, and khakis. I was bored and thinking about how dry the acid scene was back in Syracuse. So, I did the logical thing and asked these complete strangers if they knew where to score some doses. They, in turn, also did the sensible thing and said why yes, they did.

Drew was the guy with the connection, well liked around the valley for being in a band called the Shoe Crackers, which was So Cal slang for skateboarders. After smoking a joint and listening to their demo, I bought a sheet of acid—a hundred doses—of which we all ate a couple. Over the course of the night, we engaged in psychedelic shenanigans while defying a post-Rodney King Riots curfew. I came back to my sister's house in Encino as the sun rose.

My parents had booked me a cheap flight home that left on a Wednesday—the least expensive day to fly—and as a result, I missed the first three days of classes. Meanwhile, word got around school that I was bringing eighty-something hits home, and anyone who was anyone wanted to take some off my hands. So, I stuffed a baggie full of acid in my jeans pocket, and off to school I went for my first day of senior year. About twenty minutes into first period, there was a knock on the classroom door. It was Officer Sanders. I wanted to hide my stash, but I didn't have a chance. Sanders' eyes were already on me. He summoned me to follow him to Principal Williamson's office.

Williamson didn't mince words. He knew what I had and told me to cough it up. My head was running through all the articles I'd read in *High Times* about mandatory minimums. If I had the facts straight, federal law mandated that when sentencing someone, the weight of the drug's distribution method—for example, a sugar cube—was included. So, while the amount of pure liquid LSD required for thousands of doses didn't weigh enough to get you in all that much trouble, eighty hits on heavy blotter paper could get you locked up for years.

I vehemently denied having any substances on me, only a pack of cigarettes. After a few rounds of playing this game, Williamson explained that he needed parental consent to have me, a minor, searched without my permission. "But don't worry about that," he said. "I have your dad's number right here."

Williamson pulled out a piece of paper, stood up, and walked over to his phone. I looked on, trying to appear cool as a cucumber, but my head was about to explode.

"I like your shirt," Officer Sanders remarked. It was a weird thing for him to say, but then I looked down and remembered what I was wearing.

D.A.R.E to Keep Cops Off Donuts.

Sanders smiled. A moment later, Williamson extended the phone. "Your father wants to speak with you."

My dad was very direct. "Tell me now if you have anything on you, because if you say no, I'm going to let him search you."

"Yeah," I responded, trying in some way to speak code to my dad of all people.

There was a long pause. How would my father, who as far as I knew had never seen an illegal substance in his life, react?

"I'm on my way."

As we waited for my dad to arrive, Sanders and Williamson seemed to get a kick out of the fact I was about to be busted. Again, they urged me to hand over the drugs.

"I told you, I don't know what you're talking about. But, listen …" I said while pulling out my Marlboro Lights. "My parents don't know I smoke. Can I stash these over here?"

Sanders let out a snort. "You're kidding me. You're about to get busted with LSD, and you're worried about cigarettes?"

"I have no idea what you're talking about."

My dad showed up to a very tense office. On one side of the table sat Williamson and Sanders; on the other side were me and my father. I don't think anyone really wanted to speak first, but Abe broke the silence.

"Mr. Williamson," he said, "is the police officer really necessary?"

"Yes, he is. Your son is under suspicion of having some very serious drugs on him."

My dad looked at Williamson intently, but I couldn't exactly read him. Was he about to beg? Plead? Hit him in the head with a toboggan?

"Do you mind if the three of us have a moment alone?" my dad asked.

Williamson took a moment to think, then gestured for a visibly annoyed Sanders to leave the room. When he was gone, my dad pleaded his case.

"We both know E.R. is a good kid. You have bigger problems in this school than him, and if he gets arrested for drugs, it will ruin his life. Is there anything you can do?"

Williamson and my dad sat there looking one another in the eye. My heart was beating like I was on speed.

"I'll tell you what," Williamson laid out. "I'm going to step outside and have a few words with Officer Sanders. When I come back, E.R. is going to get searched. Deal?"

As he stood up, my dad and I looked at each other, aware of what Williamson had really suggested. The second we were alone, I handed my dad the acid. Five minutes later, Sanders searched me. I was clean. Williamson instructed my dad to take me home for the rest of the day, and I would be admitted back to school tomorrow.

When I got home, my dad called my mom at work to tell her what happened. Hysterical, she asked what type of drugs I had.

My dad, having not even the slightest clue, responded, "I think it was crack," and hung up the phone.

THE MORE YOU KNOW

Despite all the effort I put into passing summer school just to give myself a chance to graduate, I spent the first semester of senior year doing jack shit. If smoking weed, dropping acid, and listening to Phish were classes, I would have had straight A's. But they weren't, and I was falling behind in everything.

I heard through the grapevine that Neil Dubroff, a younger kid we had gone to Hebrew school with, was selling an extra ticket to Phish's first ever show at Madison Square Garden, December 30, 1994. Neil went to suburban JD high school, and I met him at a nearby mall to make the transaction. My parents agreed I could take the train to visit my brother Jeff in Manhattan and attend the show solo, as long as B'nai came to the city with me.

Jeff took us around New York the day of the show, and even though I was starving after all that walking, I didn't eat. I planned to find acid and wanted it to hit me as hard as possible. Once Jeff dropped me off outside the famed arena, it took me all of two minutes to find what I was looking for. A young white girl with dreadlocks and a mean-looking dog advertised her "double-dipped" hits. I assumed that was some sort of bullshit marketing gimmick, so I bought two and popped them in my mouth. Turns out, she wasn't lying about the double-dip.

I was already fucked up out of my mind when Phish came on stage and Trey repeated a deep staccato note four times. The crowd recognized it and went wild, chanting "Willllllllson" each time Trey played that pattern. This seemed to go on forever, and I had no clue why. It was all sensory overload, sending me into the hallway to find water.

There were no drinking fountains at MSG, or at least I couldn't find one, and I didn't have any money on me. Anxious, I thought focusing on the music might calm me down, so I went back inside to see the band playing "AC/DC Bag," whose line, "*brain dead and made of money, no future at all*," was fucking with my head, making me grasp the downward spiral my life was on. Graduating was an unlikely scenario, and then what the hell would I do?

Dancing like I did in Saratoga, the music took over my body. But my mind had the upper hand. Any chance I had at making it through the night rapidly disintegrated when the next song, "Sparkle," built towards its frenetic climax. As the tempo was cut in half, and half again, the band repeated "*laugh and laughing and fall apart*" over and over at a breathtaking speed. I needed air.

The path from MSG's cheap seats down to ground level consisted of several one-way escalators that were shut off during the show. Before showtime, they only went in one direction—up. But once the event started, they were turned off. At some point near the end of the night, they were turned back on again but only to go down. That wasn't such a hard concept to follow sober, but when you couldn't tell if the escalators were moving and the railings slithered like snakes, it was impossible.

It took a while—a long while—but I made it down those escalators. I was suffocating and disregarded the many signs stating "No Re-Entry." As I opened the doors, a security guard called out to reinforce that policy, but I left anyway. For about ten seconds, the air felt fresh and welcoming. Then reality set in. It was December, the temperature was five degrees, and my Dolphins Starter was inside. Wearing nothing but jeans, sneakers, and a Lollapalooza T-shirt. I quickly made my way to the front entrance, where police officers and their barricades were stationed to prevent the many ticketless fans from rushing into the show. I pushed my way through the small crowd and showed the police my ticket stub.

To the cops, I was just another fucked up kid trying to get into the show. I pleaded, explaining I needed my jacket, but these guys weren't having it. Frustrated, I walked around the area, crossing 7th Ave and turning onto a side street. There I came across a bar that from the outside looked like the perfect place to warm up. The interior seemed to take on a swanky reddish hue, while well-dressed, good-looking people gathered by the bar. Opening the door, Cool and the Gang's "Jungle Boogie," which had recently undergone a resurgence thanks to its appearance in *Pulp Fiction,* blasted through the sound system. My walk turned into a confident stride, as I brushed my flowing hair back with the bravado of John Travolta. I walked up to the bar and winked at an attractive woman while ordering a drink sure to impress—a strawberry daiquiri. But I remembered I had no money and got the heck out of there.

In a warm subway station, I stared at the turnstile, confused. I watched as others successfully made their way through, first putting tokens in a slot, which was not an option for me. But a few others jumped the turnstile, jumping being too modest of a term. These dudes had the moves down pat, walking over the metal bar effortlessly. I tried to mimic them but fell over, banging my knee right into the metal. I tried a second time and fell over. For my third attempt, I simply crawled underneath on all fours and made my way to a train already waiting in the station.

With no idea what train I was on or where it was going, my hope was I'd end up at Jeff's place. But after sitting there for who knows how long, someone told me it was out of service. Frustrated, I left, passing the turnstiles I had exerted so much energy to enter and wound up on a different corner, steam rising from a frozen manhole. My eyes followed the mist as it floated up into the sky, where it turned bright red, reflecting the neon glow of a sign that read *Peep World*. A porn shop.

The East Indian proprietors of this sex emporium paid me little mind as I stood in the doorway with bulging pupils and an acid-induced twinkle in my eyes. I was a kid in a candy store, as I went straight to one of the private coin-operated video booths and took a seat on the filthy ground, the blank glow of the TV monitor illuminating the stains, grit, and slime. Without any cash or coins, this was a futile effort, so I decided to leave. But, as I was just about out of there, a woman called out, "Hey, want to come up and play?"

I looked up to find a second-floor nook where four strippers stood, hoping to get some business in a small, curtained off area. I walked up, checking out the working girls from head-to-toe. There were two bone-skinny blondes and a thick brunette. I walked up to the bigger girl like I owned her.

"Damn, you nice and thick—just my type," I said, reaching out to touch her.

That was the first—and I was hoping only—time a woman would attempt to beat the shit out of me with the high-heel of her shoe. As she rained blows upon me, I ran towards the balcony, contemplating jumping off to commit suicide. However, I quickly calculated that at that height, I would sprain my ankle at best. So instead, I covered my head and ran out of the store.

At this point, I became fully aware that I needed medical attention, but I had no memory of taking LSD and zero idea what was wrong. Ultimately, I made the decision to go to the hospital—I bet they would have water there—and dialed 911 from a payphone. As the phone rang, I remembered where I was: New York City. No one cared about some lunatic in Times Square. But what *did* make sense to me was that they *would* come for some lost little kid, right? Who didn't love kids? So, when the 911 operator answered, I raised the pitch of my voice to imitate a small girl.

"911, what's your emergency?"

"Hi, I'm a lost little girl. Can you help me please? I'm a nine-year-old girl, and I need help."

What ensued was a jumbled conversation in which I made little sense. I struggled to even speak, let alone explain my situation. Annoyed at the operator's inability, or unwillingness, to help, I dropped the phone, where it hung by its cord. Then an epiphany struck.

Damn, Flava' Flav was right, I thought to myself. *911 is a joke.*

I strutted down the street, moving and shaking like Public Enemy's more charismatic half, singing aloud, *"Get up, a get-get down. 911 is a joke in your town."*

I walked for a few minutes singing that song, occasionally yelling, "911's a joke!" at people walking by. I didn't know if I was heading towards Jeff's, but I had definitely covered quite a bit of ground. Or, so I thought. Minutes later, I found myself right back at Peep World. The frustration of this maze was maddening. How could I get to a hospital? I ran back inside the porn shop and threw myself on the ground.

"I've been shot!" I screamed, holding my hand over my heart and wiggling around on the ground. "Call an ambulance!"

"Get the fuck out of here," the owner yelled. It was probably some of the only English he knew—a necessity in that line of work. I got up, brushed myself off, and walked out with as much dignity as possible. But after a minute or two of walking along the same damn street, I saw the bright lights of the Hotel Pennsylvania. It now seemed so obvious. If I was going to go to the hospital, there was only one way I was going to get there.

* * *

As I stood, completely exposed in the spectacularly decorated lobby, an elderly lady shrieked and a father covered his daughter's eyes. "I'm only seventeen!" I yelled, "*now* will you help me?" The answer came from two burly men in suits who grabbed my naked torso, threw me into a closet, and slammed the door.

The closet was pitch black. I didn't fully grasp where I was. I tried to leave, but someone was holding the door shut. A few moments later, the guards came back, but they hadn't found my clothes, so they threw a random trench coat on me and, as discreetly as possible, tossed me out the side door.

And just like that, I was back in the freezing cold NYC weather, now wearing nothing but some stranger's trench coat. An NYPD van was parked on the street with two cops inside, drinking coffee, so I approached the driver's side window and knocked. The officer took one look at me and spit out his drink. I motioned for him to roll down his window, as if I was asking for directions.

For the next twenty minutes, the cops stood outside the vehicle trying to figure out what was wrong with me while I squatted next to the exhaust pipe to stay warm. Eventually, an ambulance came, and as I lay down strapped to a gurney, getting my vitals taken, I looked out the back window and saw Phish fans leaving the show. I recalled the empty-eyed stares of those lost souls dancing in Saratoga. I then thought of the USY lecture we had about brainwashing cults, and it all made sense.

"We have to warn them," I pleaded with the medic.

"Warn who?"

"Them," I said, pointing to the hippies in hemp necklaces and colorful wool sweaters. "They're being turned into zombies."

As they wheeled me into the emergency room, the ultrabright lights were blinding, and the sounds of beeping monitors and patients moaning were deafening. A nurse's face appeared above my own.

"Can you tell me your name?" she asked—part of her protocol.

"E.R."

"Yes, yes. Very good, you're in the emergency room. Now can you please tell us your name?

"E.R."

"Yes, son. Very good. But what is your name?"

We went through this about four times before I arrived at a room, where an officer handcuffed me to my bed, took a seat, and read a newspaper. I turned my attention to the nurse, who was setting up various devices.

"Can I have some water?"

"Not right now, I'm sorry."

What?! I thought. That was half the reason I came here! I asked again, pleading.

"I'm sorry, you can't have water until we determine if you need surgery. We don't know what's wrong with you."

This was devastating. I motioned for her to come close, as if I had a secret to tell. The cop peered over his paper to make sure I didn't try anything funny. Curious, the nurse kneeled and gave me her ear.

"Listen," I said quietly. "Just bring me two molecules of hydrogen and one of oxygen, and don't tell nobody."

That didn't work. Glancing at my new surroundings, I noticed a roommate. He was a young black kid around my own age, and he too was restrained. He was sleeping as his distraught mother struck up a conversation with me. She explained that her son was a nice kid from a good home—a classically trained pianist who always did well in school. However, he had recently fallen in with the wrong group of kids, listening to gangster rap, smoking weed, and messing with guns.

I listened intently as she described her take on the science behind rap: how the repetitive rhythms, violent lyrics, and subliminal messaging—a term I recognized from the USY lecture—rewires your brain. According to her, this was how her son had turned into the type of person to commit armed robbery and undergo the type of marijuana-induced mania that landed him here. It was that music, she insisted, that did this to her son.

"I remember what happened to me. I remember what happened to me!" I shouted, the words "music" and "marijuana" jogging something in my brain. The nurse came back, and I explained that I'd taken lysergic acid diethylamide. That was the technical name of LSD, which I had learned at Seven Rays, but in my state, I couldn't put the acronym together—and the nurse didn't know what lysergic acid diethylamide was.

Meanwhile, the hospital staff was trying to contact my parents, and when they came upon my oldest sibling Brad's information in Scarsdale, they informed him that his son had taken some bad drugs.

"I don't think so," Brad responded, taking a look at my nephew, who was safe and sound at home. "My son's in his crib."

Eventually they located the only Jeffrey Silverbush in the NYC phonebook, and shortly after he appeared by my bedside, crying at the sight of me being handcuffed to a bed. An hour later, I was discharged.

As B'nai and Jeff took me back to his place, I bummed a smoke from my sister. It was the best fucking cigarette I'd ever had, and no other moment had provided such immense and visceral physical and psychological pleasure. Those first two drags were transcending, but when I took a third, Jeff snapped, jacking me up against a wall and screaming at me that I had to get my shit together. The cigarette had been squashed, and I didn't have the balls to break the extraordinarily fraught silence to ask for another one.

Jeff was right. I did need to get my shit together. But how? I had dug such a hole for myself that it seemed impossible. The answer came from above. Not from the heavens, but from the antiquated and barely functioning intercom in my classroom on a cold and dark winter afternoon.

* * *

"Is E.R. Silverbush in class today?" the office secretary asked my earth science teacher. "Please send him to the office." As I gathered my things, Jared and Jason, the popular kids who tossed the lingerie model on my desk in first grade, whispered that I must be in trouble yet again.

The walk to the office was always a somber occasion and too short of a journey. Usually, I pretty much knew why I was being called there, but today I had no clue. When I arrived, a secretary ushered me into Williamson's office, where my dad was sitting. Whatever it was, it was serious.

Williamson got straight down to business: He wanted me out of the school. He had no legitimate reason to kick me out, but after digging around, he discovered it wasn't possible for me to graduate. He offered to make me a deal: I drop out, and he would use his connections to allow me to take the GED test without the state mandated prep courses. And while this was far from ideal, there weren't really any other options. My father had one caveat for Mr. Williamson—he wanted to see the last of his six kids walk across the stage. So in exchange for agreeing to drop out, the principal promised I would still attend the commencement ceremony—cap, gown, and all. And that's exactly what I did, giving Williamson a huge hug as he handed me what appeared to be a diploma, but was, in reality, a GED certificate with my name spelled wrong: Edward K. Silverbush.

PARDON ME, WOULD YOU HAVE ANY?

Syracuse bids goodbye to summer each August with two weeks of the Great New York State Fair. The event, which attracts nearly a million visitors, is a spectacle of rides, fried foods, and some of the worst people watching imaginable—in the best possible way. The motley crew I was with on this late and sticky night was a prime example of that, a group of thugs, scumbags, and dropouts like myself.

Over the past few days, The Crew had disappeared one by one. Jonah, Elias, Will, Klaus, and Ryan all moved away to colleges around the northeast; Omar was living with his mom and new stepdad in Long Island; and Joe was working at Ruby Tuesdays while studying to fulfill his dream of becoming a state trooper. Technically, Shayan was still around—he was attending Syracuse University—but he was living in a dorm, and I didn't know when I'd hear from him.

As for me, I was about to start school at Onondaga Community College, or OCC. My mom had applied on my behalf and put me down as a music major, drums and percussion, because I'd been playing in that band with Elias. Our name was

Five Layer Burrito, with the other "layers" being Omar and our friend Joey Driscoll. The fifth layer? Well, that was guacamole. So yeah, the idea of my being a drum major was absurd.

With The Crew out of town, I'd been hanging with the guys from Xavier's house, including Kendall, Polish, and Tammy's little brother, Rich. Each day was exactly the same: I'd wake up and walk to their house, smoke a blunt, grab some wings, smoke some more, drink a forty of Magnum, smoke even more, and possibly get in a fight. But today, we took a long bus ride to the fair, with no agenda except to have some good old-fashioned fun. And to sell drugs. Well, that's what *I* was trying to do. In June, my grandmother had given me a thousand dollars as a "graduation" gift. Where she got that kind of money from, I didn't know, but I looked to parlay it by purchasing a blue beeper and a quarter pound of weed to sell.

By now, that quarter pound had dwindled down to one measly ounce, and I had no cash to show for it. I had smoked most of it myself. The remainder was bagged into eighths in my backpack. I hoped that among the kids trying to win goldfish and stuffed animals, there'd be people looking to score. And if I moved these last bags, I would not feel like such an asshole for wasting my grandmother's hard-earned cash. Eventually, we noticed a big dude with bloodshot eyes operating a kiddie ride. He looked like a real stoner. Not in the Phish-loving, hippie way, but in a let's get high and commit a felony kind of way. Kendall approached him on my behalf, and after some small talk, he got someone to take over the ride and motioned for me to follow him into the bathroom.

The men's room was dark and grimy. As the two of us entered a stall, I opened my backpack and asked how much he wanted. "All of it, yo," he said, snatching the bag out of my hands and taking off. I wanted to fight back, but I stood no chance, so I followed him out, hoping Xavier and them would step up. But they were near another ride, flirting with a heavy-set girl rocking coochie cutter shorts and a stroller. The guy who jacked the last of my pot was nowhere to be seen.

The walk back to the bus stop was quiet, where we all waited in silence. A nearby group of preppy dudes stood out against the sea of country farmers and junk food fanatics. One of them was Neil Dubroff, the Hebrew school kid I got my MSG ticket from. The last time I saw him, I looked totally different. With my long hair and hemp necklace, I now looked more like someone from his high school than from mine. As I said hi, the mere presence of Xavier's crew was probably freaking him out, and as I blabbered about what happened to me that night at the garden, including, "How could I not know the song *Wilson*, part of a Phish's rock opera about a society of lizards and their evil King Wilson?" I could feel Neil's friends wondering, *Who the hell is this guy?* Indeed, he looked relieved when the bus showed up.

"Ya'll Gap khaki niggas waiting for the bus, too?" Polish asked as I cringed. Neil stared, bewildered.

"Aight. Fuck you then," he finished, and our little gang boarded the bus. Grabbing a seat, I looked out the window and saw Neil's friends laughing at him as a shiny black VW pulled over to pick them up.

***

My Predator bike stood in the shed on the side of our house, untouched, for years. It was stolen on multiple occasions when I was younger, and each time my mom would spend a couple hours driving through the projects until she'd inevitably see someone riding it, yell, "That's my son's bike!" and then scoop it up after the person dropped it and fled. The BMX bike had long been out of style, but today I dusted it off for the ten-minute ride to Shai's dorm to surprise him. I didn't want to spend another single day at Xavier's.

"You're taking your bike?" my mom asked, poking her head into the shed. She always seemed to know what I was up to moments before I knew myself. I confirmed that, yes, I was, and pulled it out from under various junk that had been tossed on top of it.

"Do you know a Paul Martin?" she asked, looking down at the newspaper in her hand. "He was arrested." I ignored the question, even though I was now at the age where some of these names did ring a bell, and off I went.

Shai's dorm was on top of a steep hill owned by SU called Mount Olympus. I had passed by the road leading up hundreds of times in my life and was familiar with the signage, but I knew nothing about it other than the fact that the university's pop radio station, Z89, broadcasted from a huge antenna on top. Everyone I knew grew up on that station. But I was unaware of the two interconnected housing facilities for SU freshmen: Flint Hall and Day Hall. Flint was Shayan's new home. As I parked my bike up top and looked around, an expansive complex opened before my eyes. The lot was packed with nervous parents in expensive cars moving their overly excited children in. There were representations of every stereotypical clique imaginable—the types that existed in every 80's teen movie but were in no way reflective of my own experience. It reminded me of the opening credits of *90210*.

A member of SU's upperclassmen welcoming committee, decked out in orange and blue, saw me standing there and smiled. "Welcome to Syracuse!"

I uttered a half-hearted response and went inside the lobby and its party-like atmosphere. After looking up Shai's room number, I headed to the elevator, passing by video games like *Arkanoid*—an old favorite of mine—and *Cruis'n USA*. I noticed a group of girls who were too hot to be real. One in particular was turning the heads of students and parents alike. Her tall and slim figure was accentuated by flowing blonde hair, bright blue eyes, and a jean jacket. I hadn't seen a jean jacket in about a decade and it looked about as dated as my bike, but she had the ability to actually pull it off. I saw some mom looking incredulously at her son, and then her husband, who were both checking her out. I laughed to myself as I found the elevator.

There was no answer at Shai's door. As I stood there, thinking what to write on the white board affixed to his door—there was one on every door—a cute, skinny brunette with long brown hair walked to a room across the hall and two doors down. Her tight Rolling Rock T-shirt exposed a sliver of her navel, which was where my eyes were focused when she gave me a quick smile before going inside. Since her door wasn't locked, I tried Shai's and found that it too was open.

The concept of a dorm room was new to me, and I was shocked to see how small, organized, and demarcated it was. Shai's backpack sat on one of the beds, so I waited there until the door opened and I saw a short, meek kid with an LL Bean shirt. This was Shai's roommate, Tyler, and he was startled to see me. He looked a little uncomfortable with my presence, so after some awkward small talk, I went outside to have a smoke.

By now, many of the parents were gone, and freshmen were coming back up the stairs in droves, carrying bags of big, expensive books and various SU swag. On this beautiful August day, you could forgive them and their giddy smirks for not understanding that they'd committed themselves to a place that was essentially a frozen tundra for six months a year. While exhaling a puff of smoke through my nose, someone tapped my shoulder, and I turned, expecting to see Shai. But instead, it was a pudgy hippie who had taken my hair and dress as an invitation to strike up a conversation. His name was Lior, and he cut straight to the chase. "Hey, man. Do you know where I can get any bud?" he asked with a thick New Jersey accent.

Of course I did. And I let him know I had some on me.

"Nice!" he responded. I'd never heard that word used to convey such excitement or with such a thick accent. "Name's Lior. I'm in 224. Let's get blitzed."

* * *

Lior's room was already unpacked and decorated. Grateful Dead posters adorned his side, and a framed newspaper article announcing Jerry Garcia's recent death was the centerpiece. As I packed a bowl of my crumbly brown weed in Lior's bong, he looked disappointed.

"You can't get any kind bud?" he asked. I sort of knew what he was talking about. Kind bud was the crazy expensive, hard-to-find stuff that I'd only seen a few times, always around Deadheads or rich JD kids who hung out on Westcott. Lior was bummed I didn't know where to get any, but he shrugged it off and took a huge hit, letting out three excruciatingly loud coughs before radiating a cheek-to-cheek grin.

"Yeah, Cali harvest shouldn't be for another month or so. You should swing this shit, man, even if it is schwag. Dorms are dry." He didn't need to twist my arm. The problem was I didn't have the cash. I tried explaining this, but he didn't seem to understand.

"Go to the ATM," he said, snapping his fingers like he had just figured out the solution. He didn't know that my only bank account was the one my grandmother recently opened for me, and that I kept an actual ledger book for it. I had never even seen a bank card, let alone have one to use. Lior finally got the hint this was a financial issue, took out his dancing-bear decorated wallet, and handed me two crisp hundred-dollar bills.

"I don't need to make money, just pay me back."

As Lior took another hit, I asked about a large box labeled "lingerie." His dad, the CEO of a major women's underwear company, sent him to college with panties and bras for all the girls on his floor. I was imagining the possibilities when there was a knock on the door, and a hipster chick in a navy baby doll sundress and Doc Martens walked in.

"Natalie, meet my new best friend," he said, referring to me. "You found nugs," she excitedly noticed. "Nice!"

* * *

Lior, Natalie, and I were beyond stoned, laying in the open lawn in front of Flint Hall. She was from southern Pennsylvania, close enough to Jersey that she too said "Nice!" thirty times a day, but far enough to make her an outlier of the typical freshman from Long Island, New Jersey, or some other metropolitan suburb. I thought it was odd that no one ever said the name of their actual town. It was always "I'm from Philly" or "I'm from DC," but then I'd find out it was an hour-long train ride away.

"I am *so* glad not to be home," Lior said, his bloodshot eyes hiding behind a pair of oval Oakley sunglasses. I was jealous of their new freedom. It was a hard pill to swallow, but this college thing looked pretty cool. I turned to Natalie, who was staring at a round, yellow flier advertising some event called "The Spot." Curious, I asked about it, but Lior was quick to call it nothing but a "bunch of assholes."

"NYC-style club," Natalie read off the flier. "Bottle service only. *Dress to impress.*" She emphasized the last three words to accentuate its cheesiness.

"Like I said. Assholes," repeated Lior.

"I don't know," Natalie continued. "The promoter is a senior who used to throw big parties in the city."

"Like he said," I chimed in. "Assholes." Lior was amused.

"It's not on campus. Think there will be townies there?" Natalie asked. I had never heard the word *townie* before, but I didn't need a high school diploma to figure out what it meant. Lior looked at Natalie, like, "Shh, he is one," but she wasn't picking up on it.

"What?" she asked, aware of how Lior was looking at her. "Tell me you haven't heard stories about the townies here." Lior put his hand on his head.

"Anyway," Natalie said, turning her attention to me. "Where are you from? Let me guess," she looked me up and down. "I can't place you."

"Syracuse."

Lior was quick to break up the awkwardness. "E.R., man, I'm not gonna' lie. You seem pretty cool. So, one-for-one with townies, as far as I'm concerned."

"I agree," Natalie added, reassuring me with a grin. As I smiled back, she lifted up her sundress, revealing a pair of trashy, bright pink underwear and turned to Lior. "Check it out, I'm wearing your dad's underwear."

Lior pulled up his Oakleys to look closely. "The neon collection," he specified. "Nice."

I was staring a second too long at Natalie's bare leg when she recognized someone walking by. "Hey, I met that guy this morning," she said. "I can't remember his name, but it starts with an S." I followed her glance to see Shayan coming back from the bookstore. He looked in our direction and squinted to make out if that was really me. "E.R.?" he asked as he approached us.

Natalie looked confused. "You guys know each other?"

* * *

Shai and I grabbed snacks from the vending machine using his meal plan, and after catching up, he went to his last orientation sessions of the day. While he was out, I picked up an ounce of weed from a connection on Westcott, bagged it up, and sold it to people on Lior's floor. Now Shai was back, and the two of us were in front of Flint, smoking cigarettes. While the sun set over Mount Olympus, we watched the dorm scene unfold like tourists in our own town.

Out on the grassy area, freshmen were throwing footballs and frisbees, and three hippie kids who looked fresh off Dead tour—Mitch, Sean, and Corey—were playing hacky sack. The day's last bit of sunshine made the dozens of new SUVs in the parking lot sparkle. I hadn't heard that the glorified minivan had become cool, and I couldn't understand how so many students afforded one. I thought college kids were supposed to be broke—my siblings and their friends had all been—but it looked like these kids had more money than any parents I knew.

As Shai and I lit up stogs, he explained that The Mount, especially Flint, was considered the best freshman dorm by far. And since his dad worked at the university, he pulled strings to get him assigned here. I was wondering if that was a good thing or bad thing when a black Ford Explorer pulled into an empty space right in front of us. The Rolling Rock girl I saw in Shai's hallway stepped out of the passenger seat.

"Oh shit. Watch this," he said. Shai clearly knew her, but I wasn't sure about the curly- haired guy who came out of the driver's seat a moment later.

"That her man?" I ask.

"He wishes." That was exactly the answer I was hoping for as the two came our way.

"Shayan!" Rolling Rock girl was happy to see him, and he gave me a quick, boastful look to ensure I noticed.

"Hey, this is my boy from home, E.R. E, this is Samantha and Matt."

"You're from Syracuse too?" Matt asked in a way that didn't sit well. I ignored him and turned to Samantha.

"And you're from …?" I asked her.

"The city," she responded cheerfully.

"New York?"

"Is there any other?"

"Okay, so are you actually from the city? Cause it seems like everyone here says they are from some city, but they're really from the sticks."

She smiled, admitting, "I'm from New Jersey, but …" "I knew it!"

"Wait! But, right outside the city. Fifteen minutes away."

"Ummmhmmm," I let out as she laughed. Shai didn't like what he saw; Matt looked even more annoyed. My beeper went off, cutting through the awkwardness.

"You're blowing up, kid," Shai commented.

"Yeah. I think Lior gave my number to half the campus," I explained while putting the device back in my pocket.

"Wait, are you *that* E.R.?" Samantha asked. Shai looked even more bewildered than me.

"Is there any other?" My response made her smile. In the periphery, I saw Shai wince.

"A beeper. Wow," Matt said, inserting himself into the conversation. I figured it wasn't hard to remember the name E.R., especially as the only dude around with weed. But I must have been visibly annoyed with Matt's condescending tone, because Shai stepped in to diffuse the situation.

"Matt's from LA," he said, trying to forge some sort of connection between the two of us. "Do you know a guy named …" He turned to me. "What's that guy's name, the dude with the sheet of acid?"

"Drew," I said. Shai was referring to the Shoe Crackers guy. Did he really think there was only one person named Drew in all of LA?

"Drew from the Shoe Crackers?" Matt asked. I couldn't believe it. After a couple of what-a-small-world comments, Matt and Samantha headed inside.

"Can I call you sometime?" I blurted out to Sam. Shai and Matt looked surprised by this, but not as surprised as when she gave me her number. I wrote it down on my pack of Marlboro Lights.

I felt victorious on my way home, but that euphoria was short-lived. When I went to get my bike, it was gone. I hoped my mom wouldn't notice.

JUST SAY NO

As I slowly opened my eyes, specks of dust danced above, finding their way between the beams of light that poked through hundred-year-old window frames. I had woken up on this bed pretty much every day of my life, but today it looked different. The Looney Toons wallpaper and shelves of old stuffed animals betrayed a sense of stagnated adolescence. I thought of my new friends on The Mount and my long-held notion that caring about school and enjoying life were incompatible with one another. Then I saw Samantha's number on my smokes. It made me forget that my life was heading down the toilet, until my mom's frantic voice pierced the air.

"Your bike's gone!"

I tried for about twenty minutes to convince her to let it go, but my mom insisted on going to find it. I didn't tell her the truth—that it was not in the hood. That the most likely scenario was some idiot SU student was using it for beer runs. But she was having none of that. She grabbed her car keys, and as she drove over to the projects, I got myself ready for my first day at Onondaga Community College.

The Mount was a tough act to follow. Every single thing about the OCC campus was disappointing. There were no dorms, the parking lot was full of clunkers, and good-looking girls were few and far between. While some were serious students who were unable to afford a better school, or adults hitting their second stride in life, most were fuckups. The county had given the school its tired, its poor, its huddled-in-the-rain-to-light-a-joint masses—an assemblage of local high school burnouts. And nowhere was this truer than in the music department.

"Take a look at the person to your left, and then at the person to your right," were the first words my music history professor expressed to the class. It was eight in the morning, and none of us were fully awake. On my left was a bespectacled girl with a flute case; on my right, a long-haired dude wearing a hemp necklace who looked, well, a little like me. We gave each other a knowing nod.

"I've been doing this long enough to know that one of those two people will not be here at the end of the semester," the professor continued. "So, my wise words to you are, come to class and pay attention. I know that Gregorian chants might not be the most thrilling thing, but this is important material." I wondered what the hell a Gregorian chant was.

When class ended, the hippie kid introduced himself. His name was Jake McCallistair. He graduated from JD, the same suburban school that MSG-ticket-Neil went to.

"What class you got next?"

I pulled a schedule out of my pocket to check. "Physical Conditioning."

"Gym?" He laughed. "Fuck that, let's go get high in my car."

The inside of Jake's fifteen-year-old Ford Escort was a world removed from The Mount. As he went on and on about weed, acid, and Phish, I saw him as the JD version of me. At first, this statement popped into my head with no specific connotation, but as Jake cashed his bowl out the window and put his hair in a ponytail, I saw myself in a new light. And I didn't like it.

* * *

Even though I was eighteen, I didn't have a driver's license. So my only options for commuting to OCC were a two-hour bus trip or an early morning ride in my dad's red van followed by a return trip at five. I chose the latter, and by the end of that first day, I was beat. But after a shower and a change of clothes, I was re-energized and ready for a date with Samantha.

I walked up to The Mount in my nicest clothes, a wrinkled button-down flannel shirt with corduroy pants, and my hair in a ponytail. But before getting to Sam's room, I had to stop by Day Hall to make a sale to some Freshman named Craig. He did a double take when I arrived, sure that we'd met before. But he couldn't recall how. I had no clue who he was, but when he pieced it together and said "Pez!" I noticed the same lazy eye that tripped me out last summer at SPAC. He was that friend of Elias' sleepaway camp buddy we had met up with.

Excited to see a familiar face and fellow Phish fan, Craig sat me down at his computer. He was on the internet—something I had never seen in person—in an AOL chat forum for Phish fans.

The rumor going around was one I refused to believe that people actually bought into: Phish would be playing Michael Jackson's *Thriller* album on Halloween.

Craig appreciated that while I was passionate about the band, I knew so little of their music. He explained that last year Phish donned a "musical costume" on Halloween, performing The Beatles *White Album* in its entirety, along with two full Phish sets. They were repeating that concept this year at the Rosemont Horizon in Chicago. While the album was a secret, the internet —and Craig—said it would be none other than *Thriller*. It was one of the most ridiculous things I'd ever heard, but while he and I disagreed on the likelihood of that happening, we became immediate friends and made a pact to do whatever it took to get to that show. But first, I had a date.

When I knocked on Samantha's door, it was her roommate, Kara, who answered. Dressed in a flowing black skirt, golden tank top, and with long, straight reddish-blonde hair, she exuded a blend of hipster feminism that would have been right at home at a Lilith Fair festival. She was a hundred percent attitude, forgoing any hello or other niceties. She simply let me in and went back to sketching on her bed. In the back, Samantha was applying her last bit of lipstick. She smiled and turned to me.

"Hey you!" The way she said this, innocently yet with verve, grabbed me. "Ready?" she asked, grabbing her purse. As we left, Kara called out.

"By the way, Luke called."

"Okay, thanks," Samantha responded. I spent the entire walk from her room to the lobby wondering who the hell Luke was. A moment later, we were in front of Flint and she was scanning the parking lot. "Where are you parked?" she asked.

"I actually don't have a car."

"Really?!" She seemed shocked. "So we're taking a cab?"

"Well, it's a nice night and it's not that far. I thought we could walk. Isn't that what you New Yorkers do, anyway?"

She grinned. "We take cabs."

I hadn't thought this arrangement would be unusual or unexpected, and I was fairly certain it was a short walk. But now I was acutely self-conscious about the whole thing. But any doubt I had about Sam's reaction was immediately alleviated with an enthusiastic, "Okay!"

Forty-five minutes later, I realized the walk to downtown's Armory Square was much farther than I thought. I was beginning to worry I'd blown the whole thing when we arrived at the recently revitalized area. In the past year or two, a dozen bars, shops, and restaurants had sprung up seemingly overnight.

Samantha's face lit up when walked past a candy shop with a window display full of Jelly Bellies. The innocence in her voice seemed dissonant with the face and body of someone with the power to bring most men to their knees. She was more in place when we got to Style High, a club-like bar that was owned by Mike, a friend of my Five Layer bandmate Driscoll's dad. And the two times I'd been there, I was able to drink without ID. I was hoping that would still be the case.

Sitting in a back booth drinking wine, we told high school stories and spoke of our new lives—well, her life—on the Mount. When "The Spot" and its now ubiquitous yellow flier came up, I didn't mention it was the cheesiest thing ever. I fully expected her to be looking forward to it. But when she expressed how lame she thought it was, I knew this was the chick for me. And when the bill came, I didn't want to leave. The vibration of my beeper reverberated throughout our booth, and I took a look to see who it was.

"So, you're like a big man on campus?" she said, playfully but impressed. I couldn't tell her it was actually my parents. While I never had a curfew, they generally wanted me home around eleven or so. And despite my seventeen-year history of disobedience, I stuck to that time the best I could out of respect for my dad. He was adamant that every time I came home, Cholo would wake him up, and it would be impossible to fall back asleep.

I put the beeper back in my pocket and pulled out a wad of crumpled up bills to pay the check. As I counted, Sam stared. "I should have stopped at the ATM," she said apologetically. Before I had a chance to react, a loud voice behind my shoulder interrupted.

"What are you doing here?!" It was Mike, the owner. He was tall with a deep, authoritative voice and a brown goatee. As he approached our booth, it wasn't clear if he was happy to see us or mad that his bartender had served minors. But when he smiled, shook my hand, and waited for an introduction to Samantha, I knew we were all good. After some small talk, he walked over to the bar and produced a stack of free passes to their legendary weekly disco night, inviting us to bring as many SU students as we could. I didn't need him to explain they were his best customers. Then, seeing the sad display of crumpled up cash on the table, he told me not to worry about the check.

As Samantha and I began the walk home, we were both lost in thought when dark, deep clouds rolled in. There was no doubt it was going to start pouring at any moment. After a few moments, Sam finally spoke. "Can I ask you something?"

"Sure."

"Why don't you have a car?"

"I don't have a license."

"Ummm, that's crazy. Why?"

The truth was I never saw the point. There was no way I could afford a car.

"I don't really know. But my parents are convinced it's because I got caught driving without a license, and that I'm, like, banned from getting one until I'm twenty-one."

"Did you?"

"No, but it's what they think. For two years, my mom checked the police blotter for proof."

As we laughed, a burst of lightning lit up the sky, and it began to pour. This only caused us to laugh even harder as our clothes and hair became fully soaked. It was the worst moment to ask the question in the back of my head, but I had to know who Luke was.

"My boyfriend," she said matter-of-factly.

"Oh."

"But I'm going to break up with him … I think."

"You think?"

As she searched for a response, I went in and kissed her. But the rain came down even harder, so we made a run for it. The last thing she said when I dropped her off in front of Flint was that she couldn't wait to see me again, and not to tell anyone we kissed.

"Not even Shayan!" she specified, yelling through the rain and wind.

"Not even Shayan!" I yelled back.

* * *

"You Shear beer bear?" was the first question Shai asked me when I told him I hooked up with Samantha. He was a little envious.

"Nah, chicka frown down."

He seemed relieved. "And she has a man?"

"Hmmhmm."

"Well, fuck it, let's smoke a bowl," was the best consolation Shai could offer. I didn't think he had ever offered anyone weed. He never had it. I was the pothead, and he the drinker. Something was up, and when he asked how my dealing was going—he knew damn well I was barely making any money—it was obvious where he was going with this. And I didn't like it.

"Two words," he said. "Johnny Sabs."

I hoped he was kidding about the guy we last saw tasing someone at Xavier's. But he was serious. "Uh, two words: in-sane."

"I need loot, man. I went out to the bars last night with a bunch of people. Shit gets expensive. Drinks were five dollars. And

I want to be able to, you know, buy drinks for girls and all that."

I nodded and took another hit.

"I'm going to rush," he then let out, as if confessing a deep secret.

"Rush who?" I asked. I thought he meant fighting.

"No, rush. It's a fraternity thing."

I couldn't understand why anyone, let alone Shai, would want to be in a frat. They personified the words cheesy, corny, and lame.

Shai didn't necessarily disagree. "Bro. I'm trying to fuck," was his rationalization. He was convinced that to get the real SU experience, and by that he meant slutty girls and crazy parties, you needed to be in a house. And the one he had his eye on was Delta Uphalson, AKA DU, known to many as "drugs unlimited." And he thought access to large quantities of weed would help him get in.

"They gonna' spank your ass with a paddle?" I asked. I was only half kidding.

"I don't know, maybe."

"Why don't I just pick up an ounce on Westcott?"

"We need more than that."

"I can get it."

"And we need it fronted."

And there it was: the worst idea ever, from the mouth of my best friend. I thought about the severity of the proposition. Borrowing weed from Johnny could be a dangerous mistake. But I also thought about that crumbled up wad of cash I threw down on the table last night. It *was* embarrassing.

"If we fuck up, a fraternity paddle will be the least of our problems."

"I know."

"Even if Johnny Sabs says okay, how can we move it? He's going to want his money right away."

"I know a couple people."

* * *

One of the guys Shai had in mind to introduce us to customers was a Day Hall freshman named Kyle Staples, or just Stapes. A week prior during student housing orientation, Shai and a couple hundred of his cohorts had to endure a painful session that included an in-depth lecture about how under no conditions, whatsoever, was drinking allowed in the dorms. The resident advisors had finished beating a dead horse, emphasizing this last point ad nauseam, when a hand went up all the way in the back of the hall. Stapes, a skinny kid in a Red Sox hat and thick Boston accent, had a question.

"What about pot?"

After that session, Shai approached him and said that he had a weed connection, and the two of us were introduced. The experience threw me for a loop.

"Let's go to my rum and smoke a bowl," was the first thing he said to me.

"I'm sorry, what?" I was having a hard time understanding what the hell he was saying.

"My rum. I got some wicked dank bud, so let's go to my rum and smoke a fahking bowl."

"Oh, your *room*," I corrected.

"That's what I said, my rum."

I followed Stapes to his Celtics-decorated room over, where we met up with Shai, lazy-eye Craig, and Stapes' buddy Steve Chipetta, also known as Petta. He was a good-looking guy with icy blue eyes and the only freshman I'd met so far who didn't get high. As he put on some Pearl Jam, Craig cradled a large suede pouch like a baby, pulling out a psychedelic-colored glass pipe that looked like something from the Middle Ages. Stapes and Craig admired it in awe, but the significance was lost on me. After asking about it, the two seemed incredulous that I was unaware of Jerome Baker's legendary hand-blown glass bongs. When I was told it cost three hundred dollars, I was floored.

As we passed the pipe around, exhaling through an empty roll of toilet paper stuffed with fabric softener to mask the smell, Stapes rattled off names of potential clients from other dorms. As he handed out bowls of Frosted Flakes in paper bowls, we engaged in the type of heavy intellectual debate that took place in dorm rooms all across the country: who were the hottest girls in the dorm? Samantha's name came up, at which point Shai gave me a sly look. But there was a firm consensus that the girl in the jean jacket—I wasn't the only one to take note of her wardrobe—was our crown jewel. It wasn't only that dad who fantasized about getting in her pants. Everyone did.

"Does anyone actually know her name?" Shai asked. None of us did.

"Jenny," Petta informed us. Well, one of us knew her name, at least.

As I wondered *how* Petta knew her name, Stapes blurted out, "Jean Jacket Jenny!" We all cracked up at this nickname, and Craig got up to change the tunes. But when Petta spotted a Phish tape, he put a stop to it. Turned out Petta didn't just not like Phish, he *really* did not like Phish. Hate would have been too strong of a word because while he couldn't tolerate their music, he had a curiosity in how obsessed their fans were.

Petta had seen many of his high school buddies burn out on pot and become people who lived on tour. That led to my recounting that crazy night I had in the city during the MSG show, and he said he wasn't surprised to hear it. He thought Phish purposely fucked with their fans and cited our quest to go to the Halloween show as a prime example of this. He could not understand why we would be willing to—if we were able to find tickets—leave school to drive to Chicago for a concert.

"Dude, it's going to be wicked awesome. Thriller!" Stapes exclaimed, pointing to a poster on his wall for the forthcoming show. It featured a scrawny, young hippie being attacked by a school of fish and running for his life. Before I could protest at how stupid the whole *Thriller* rumor was, there was a knock on the door. We began the routine of hiding all of the paraphernalia and spraying Uzo air freshener, but by the second knock, Stapes was already at the peephole.

"Petta, it's for you," he called out.

Petta lived on an entirely different floor, so it was odd someone would come looking for him. What was even more unbelievable was that it was none other than Jean Jacket Jenny. Petta got up and left with her, leaving us to stare with our mouths open. That's when Stapes offered the explanation "Fahking chicks love Petta."

That part was now painfully obvious, as we all sat in awe.

"So," Stapes began. "When you getting this weed?"

* * *

Oakwood Cemetery was a 250-year-old graveyard directly adjacent to The Mount. During the day, its sprawling hills evoked the English countryside, while at night the old tombstones and large, twisted trees recalled the 1980's film *Poltergeist*. That film, which my older sister B'nai made me watch at age five, still frightened me. But I was even more scared of Johnny Sabs, the person Shai and I came here to meet on this cold and windy night.

The purpose of this meeting was to discuss our business proposition, but something made me feel like we were waiting for the grim reaper. Shai and I had been at the same party as Johnny Sabs twice since we first saw him under the strobe light at Xavier's, so he had no problem taking the meeting. He too had been looking to penetrate the freshman market.

When Johnny Sabs' notorious dark purple Mercury Cougar approached on the gravel road with its lights off, Shai and I took a deep breath. The car came to a stop inches from our feet. We waited for Johnny to get out, but he just sat there, engine running. Finally, he turned the car off and rolled his window down.

"Well ... ya'll getting in or what?"

Shai was quick to get in back, leaving me to sit beside the infamous dealer, but as soon as I opened the front door—

"Nah, homie, get in back."

A moment later, we were in the back of the car, and Johnny was staring at us from his rearview mirror.

"So, what's up?" he asked.

"Uhhhuhhhh." Shai could barely get a word out he was so nervous.

"Ya'll tryin' to sling for me?"

I tried to intervene. "Uhhh …" But I couldn't offer much more than Shai.

"What, ya'll niggas like Beavis and Butthead or somethin'?"

Shai and I looked at each other, wondering if we had somehow pissed the man off. Then Sabs bursted into laughter.

"Uhhh. Uhhhh," he imitated us, cracking himself up. Nervously, we laughed along with him, until suddenly his mannerism turned deadly serious.

"Ya'll know I'mma have to fuck you up, right?"

Wait, what just happened? I wanted to simply ask, "What?" but I was so nervous all I could muster was, "I beg your pardon?"

"Two weeks. One G. If you don't pay my ass on time, I'mma have to fuck you up."

"Oh, yeah, yeah, for sure," Shai and I said, almost in unison, relieved that the situation was only hypothetical. Then Johnny turned around for the first time, and we truly grasped the magnitude of his presence. He handed us a black trash bag.

"I'll be in touch. Peace."

"Um, so, like when will you need—"

"I said peace."

We got out of the Cougar, and he was off. Once Johnny's tail lights were reduced to a tiny red speck, we relaxed. Shai opened the bag and his mouth dropped.

"Holy shit, that's a lot of herb."

COKE IS IT

The polyester bell bottoms I dug out of a closet were too tight, but I just had to wear them. Inspired by Andy Warhol with Coca-Cola logos all over, I couldn't believe my brother Brad used to wear them out twenty years ago. Samantha, in her 70's-inspired makeup and hairstyle, agreed they were awesome. The two of us were in the back of a cab on our way to disco night at Style High.

As we breezed past the bouncer, Mike the owner gave me a high five. The band, named The Electric Chick Magnets, was playing "Kung Fu Fighting" to a packed crowd. We walked over to Shai, who was talking to the always-stylish Natalie and her Flint neighbor Seth, whose huge hemp necklace was partially hidden by a dyed-green goatee. A moment later, a dozen or so kids from The Mount rushed over to greet the men of the hour: us. It had only been a few days since Shai and I had met with Johnny Sabs, but freshmen from all over campus were buying our weed. It was our first time hanging off-campus, and it was the perfect place to celebrate.

Dancing with Samantha later in the night, it became obvious to all that something was going on between us. It was especially clear to Matt, who pretended not to care but kept glancing in our direction. His curly hair, poofed into a Jewfro for the occasion, matched his partially exposed chest. I moved in closer to Samantha, but she made a gesture that told me *people know I have a boyfriend*. I eased up, and when the song was over, I went to get drinks.

The bar was crowded and intimidating. Unsure how to proceed, I imitated the dudes gathered around me, who were holding out large bills in hopes the scantily dressed bartender would serve them next. Figuring that a crisp hundred would get her attention, I took one out, pushed my way up to the bar, and waited until eventually she came over. The problem was I had no idea what to order. I looked over at the group next to me, six girls taking shots, and asked what they were drinking.

"Kamikazes," she had to scream over the noise.

I didn't know what that meant, but I asked for twelve of them, much to the annoyance of the dude in line next to me. When a tray of shots was placed down, I handed the bartender the hundred-dollar bill, expecting change. Instead, she said I was twenty short. Shit that was a lot of money.

"I know Mike," I said, hoping the owner card would work.

"Cool," she said indifferently. "He left." Dejected, I handed her another twenty. She stood there for a moment before giving me an angry look and walking away.

"You gotta tip her, bro," a voice behind me said. It was Paulie, a short and stocky Italian American freshman in head-to-toe Tommy Hilfiger and slick-backed hair. I only knew three things about Paulie: His favorite movie was Goodfellas, his father was a well-known surgeon in Albany, and he drove a brand new S500, which I was told was top of the line Mercedes. I reluctantly put yet another twenty on the bar and picked up the tray as he spoke into my ear.

"You can't get any kind bud, just that shit Mexican weed?" he asked. I explained what some hippie kids told me, which I wasn't sure was true, that there were harvest issues in California. In a normal September, phenomenal pot would have already arrived by the pound.

"Go take those shots, and let's talk. I want to run something by you and your boy," Paulie continued with the manner of someone desperate to be seen as mafioso. I then walked over to The Mount peeps and watched a hundred and forty dollars' worth of liquid dribble down their chins. As the band began to play ABBA's "Dancing Queen", I glanced at Samantha on the floor, who smiled at me.

"Yo," said Shai, who suddenly appeared with his arm on my shoulder. "Paulie wants us to get him a sheet of acid. Can you hook me up with Benji?"

So that's what Paulie was talking about. I hadn't spoken to Benji since he got me those Felix the Cat hits for the Westcott Acid Test over a year ago. But I nodded, gave Shai a fist bump, and went out to dance.

* * *

I took my time undressing Samantha, looking her in the eyes as I took off her shirt and cupped a breast. I had dreamt about this moment for weeks, and now it was actually happening.

"What about Luke?" I asked as I moved my hands to her zipper.

"Who?" she said with a mischievous grin. And as we continued undressing each other, there was a loud knock on the door that snapped me back to reality. I was in a music practice room at OCC. Alone. With the lights off. With my dick in my hand.

I thought back to the disco night we went to just a day ago. Sam wanted me over at her place after, but, as she explained, Kara would be there. And, besides, my parents had been paging me. I kicked myself the entire way home. Frustrated, I got into bed when my pager vibrated. The number just said "99," but I knew it was Samantha, and I knew what it meant: It was beeper code for nighty night.

And now here I was in a practice room fantasizing when the sound of the door unlocking cut through the silence. I pulled my pants up, bolted to the piano bench, and began to play whatever came to mind to make it look like I was doing *anything* other than jerking off. When the lights came on, I saw the flute girl from my music history class standing there with another girl, their mouths agape.

"I like to practice in the dark," I blurted while banging away on the keys, the instrument hiding my undone belt. "I get better that way."

"I'm so sorry ... we had this reserved, and it was locked, so we got the key ..." she awkwardly offered, possibly more embarrassed than I was.

"Just give me a minute to finish up," I frantically let out. I pretended not to hear her while continuing to play like my life depended on it. Finally, they shut the door.

Even though it was already mid-September and the semester was in full motion, I had been to each of my classes exactly two times. I spent most of my time smoking stogs outside the student center with various stoners or getting high with Jake McCallistair in the parking lot. But today, I decided to actually show up for my private drum lesson—once I had a cup of coffee and another cigarette. Taking a drag, my mind wondered how I even ended up here in the first place. Not at OCC, I knew how *that* happened, but as a drummer.

5 Layer Burrito's first gig was during the fall of '94—a full year ago—at open mic night at Zopie's, a coffee shop on the SU campus that high school kids also frequented. It happened to be the same night as another one of those USY events, this time in Syracuse, and my dad was outraged I wasn't going. But that didn't stop my mom from hosting a kid in town from Poughkeepsie. This was a ludicrous proposition because the kids who came to these things were not the type of kids to appreciate my neighborhood. Or my house. Or my killer dog.

"But you had such a nice time at the last one," my mother recalled. That was partly true, but only because I got high as a fucking kite. But it was too late; CeCe had already made the arrangement. We picked up Scott, a quintessentially nice Jewish boy, at the train station and stopped off at my dad's shop to bring him lunch.

Silverbush Upholstery was in a neighborhood where shop owners like my dad scrubbed off graffiti on a regular basis. It was where he fended off attackers during the 1960's race riots. And now it was an area that was scaring the crap out of this poor kid from Poughkeepsie. After my dad cracked some lame joke along the lines of "I thought E.R. asked for a girl to stay over. Who's this?" we made our way to Westcott street.

I was embarrassed just to have Scott step foot in our house, but after Cholo nearly took his nose off, I was counting the hours until the open mic night. I didn't have to wait that long, though. Poughkeepsie Scott asked to use the phone, and a few minutes later, USY found him a new place to stay.

I knew the drive to Zopie's with my dad would be tense given all that had taken place, but what I didn't anticipate was a massive argument about my hair. By now it was down to my shoulders, and it drove my father crazy. I had gotten this lecture dozens of times, but tonight it was delivered with such conviction and anger that I knew it wasn't really about my hair. The hostility was really about the USY event, and when I brought that up, he went on a diatribe about the importance of my Judaism. The argument escalated until we pulled up in front of Zopie's.

And as I sat there pretending to listen, I watched the college students in line to get into Harry's, an SU bar directly above Zopies. I walked by this bar many times and never understood it. Didn't this crowd with its hair gel, sparkly jewelry, tacky clothes, and horrid music know how God awful cheesy they were?

A DOSE OF REALITY

After a full minute of my dad's tirade, I snapped and said something that I knew would push him over the edge, that wasn't at all true, and that I was sure I'd regret. The words "Who gives a fuck about being Jewish?" came out of my mouth, then I stormed out of the car with my conga drum and walked towards Zopie's. Coolio's "Fantastic Voyage" was blaring out of Harry's, and I was thinking about how much I hated that song when, *bam*, someone slapped the shit out of me. I looked up to find my dad standing there with a look in his eye that was full of rage, yet sympathetic. As blood dripped down my nose and the Harry's cheeseballs stared, I gathered my composure, collected my drum, and went inside for the open mic.

Sitting outside the student center remembering that night, my cigarette had burned down without a single drag. I lit another one and thought back to Sam. I wanted to know where I stood. After running through various scenarios in my head, someone mentioned they were off to class. I realized I would be late to my lesson and decided to put it off for another week.

* * *

Hours after coming home from OCC, my dad gave me a ride to The Mount. It was a year after the Zopie's incident, and while my hair was now even longer, he had given up on getting me to cut it, although his glances never failed to express his thoughts. As we pulled up to Flint Hall in the Silverbush Upholstery van, a group of impossibly done-up girls in knee-high boots, revealing clothes, and shiny, almost plastic-looking skin, were in the lobby waiting for cabs. It didn't go unnoticed by Abe.

"Now I know why you come here all the time," he said with a smile.

I didn't want to let him down by saying that these chicks couldn't have cared less who I was, nor did I want to know them. Or that tonight was The Spot and while these girls would be getting shitfaced and making fools of themselves at a ridiculously corny club, I would be dropping acid and hanging out in a rock quarry. Shai had bought a ten-strip of acid from Benji to test out what we'd be selling Paulie. Each dose had the word "magic" stamped on it, and it was an apt description because they were, well, fucking magical. And they made Syracuse University Research Park feel surreal.

Research Park was a long-abandoned rock quarry frozen in time. It was situated on top of SU's south campus, a huge hill a couple miles from the main quad that consisted of townhome-like student housing for sophomores and graduate students. Farther up was an indoor ice skating rink, tennis complex, dining hall, some administrative offices, and if you kept going and knew where to head into the woods, the dilapidated quarry. A couple years ago, someone from Nottingham discovered this place, and it became a new spot for keg parties.

By the time our group walked up, the acid was hitting us hard and the quarry's dried riverbed and rolling dirt hills presented a Martian-like landscape. Alongside me and Shai were Samantha, her roommate Kara, Matt Reynolds, Natalie, and two of her friends—Erin, a bubbly blonde from Miami in head-to-toe

DKNY gear, and Carla, a freckled redhead who was equally stylish. Shai also brought along a classmate from a different dorm named Lamar. He was a light-skinned dude from Queens who wore an Adidas track suit and reminded me of a mannequin at DeJaiz or Chess King. The only one of us not tripping, he held a forty of St. Ives in his hands.

Shai was up front leading the way even though he was barely capable of standing. Kara was in back, lost in her own head and looking melancholy. Samantha was next to her and looked similarly in deep thought, while I struggled to find my balance on one of the many dunes. In reality, the mound was not that steep and the drop not that far. But looking down, all I saw was a deep abyss interrupted by an occasional meteorite—I was hallucinating big time. Afraid to fall into space, I sat down and refused to budge until a hand gently cupped my shoulder.

"Hey you," Samantha said, with what I now considered to be her trademark phrase. "Come on. It's only a hill." Her smile snapped me back to reality, and a wave of confidence rushed through my body. We hadn't kissed since that night in the rain, although the nature of our last date probably didn't help things.

I had taken her to the Westcott movie theater where we saw *Kids*. The film about young teens getting STD's wasn't exactly fodder for romance. But we had an amazing time, and if I had my own place—or if Kara wasn't her roommate—something probably would have happened. And looking up at her now, her hair waving in psychedelic patterns, I decided now was the time to tell her to ditch Luke.

"Let's move." The moment was ruined by Reynolds' brash voice behind us. While he frowned at his now-scuffed white sneakers, Sam helped me up. With the rest of the guys right behind us, any grand speeches would have to wait. As we continued along the path, the ground seemed to shake beneath my feet. For a moment I thought it was an earthquake, but it was only my beeper. I was sure it was my parents, so I ignored it.

After a long trek down to the quarry floor, we reached a series of abandoned buildings reminiscent of a western ghost town. Sitting among the ruins of an abandoned shack, Lamar attempted to hit on Natalie *and* Carla, to no one's delight. I packed a bowl and passed it around, hoping the distraction would allow me to pull Sam aside. The moon had not yet come out yet, and several stars were visible, a rarity in Syracuse. I stood up and headed to Sam, but Erin excitedly yelled that a bright red dot in the sky was Mars, causing everyone to turn and look. I didn't mention it was only the radio tower on top of The Mount.

"Paulie is going to be very happy with his sheet," I said to Shai, who nodded in agreement. Meanwhile, as Erin stared into the sky, her voice grew even louder. "I feel like we're in Star Wars," she said. "Luke, I am your father."

That name—Luke—hung in the air like the sound of a ballerina falling on stage. Everyone was silent as Samantha got up and walked away. Carla tried to break the tension by asking if I lived in Flint or Day.

"He lives with his parents," Reynolds answered before I even had a chance to process the question. Carla seemed confused by that statement.

"He doesn't go to school here," he clarified, somehow making everything even more awkward. But if his comment was meant to belittle me, it didn't work. Those who didn't know this already thought it was hilarious. The laughter provided a window for me to go talk to Sam. but a hand on my knee indicated for me to stop. It was Kara.

"Give her some space," she said. I took the advice, really more of a command, and went to pack yet another bowl, but my bag was empty. As I wondered how we'd smoked so much, the conversation turned to how lame of an event The Spot was. And while everyone took turns mocking it, I saw how ragged my clothes were compared to everyone else. I glanced at Kara, who seemed to be thinking as intensely as I did whenever I tripped—going all the way back to the stream behind Elias' house. In that moment I sensed a real kinship with her, despite the fact that she didn't like me.

"Don't you wish you could think like this all the time?" I asked, positive she knew exactly what I was talking about.

"Like what?" she answered, deflating the temporary connection I thought we had. She seemed offended. I thought about how to articulate it. Smart? No, that's not it. Curious? No, not quite. Annoyed, Kara got up and walked away, and that's when I noticed Samantha was no longer alone. Reynolds was with her.

"They together?" Lamar asked, suddenly in my ear. I didn't answer, but the question bothered me enough to approach them. Reynolds quickly made an excuse about having to pee, and now was my chance to tell her how I felt. It was now or never, but as I opened my mouth and struggled with what to say, she got her words out first.

"I'm going home this weekend," she said, my confidence now shot. The worst part was she didn't say why. Was it to break up with Luke? To fuck him? I had so many questions. But a simple, "Okay," was all I was able to get out before we rejoined the crowd. As I sat, Erin handed me my cashed bowl. When I put it in my pocket, I got a paper cut. It was a flier for The Spot. Holding it up for all to see, the moonlight caused the shiny gold cardboard to seem luminescent. It gave us the creeps.

Carla jokingly yelled, "Put it away, it's burning my eyes!"

"Such a joke," Natalie said about the flier. "I'm going down to the city for a real party in a couple weeks." "What party?" Erin asked.

"A rave," Natalie said, suggesting that should have been obvious.

"Why didn't you just say rave?" Erin continued.

"Because no one calls them that."

"Everyone says that."

"Yeah, but not people who actually go to parties."

"You mean raves."

As I put the flier back in my pocket, the words "dress to impress" stood out to me, especially since I'd been wearing the same pair of jeans for the past week.

* * *

The 900 block of Westcott was damp and quiet at one in the morning. Still tripping, though well off my peak, I was walking home. As the mossy trees and their impossibly long branches protruded over the streetlights, I envisioned the forest that consumed this land hundreds of years ago, and all the blood, sweat, and tears that tamed it.

My footsteps reverberated with every step, punctuated by birds, squirrels, and the faint bumping of a subwoofer in the distance. Walking up my porch steps, the creaking sounds of the hundred-plus old stairs disrupted the evening calm. As soon as I entered, Cholo let out a piercing bark but quickly picked up my scent and licked my hand. My father sat at the dining table, his silhouette barely visible in the darkness. He didn't look angry, just tired and defeated.

"E.R.," he said, his accent thicker from exhaustion. "I don't know what to do with you." He glanced at my long hair. "What are you going to do with your life? Be a drummer?" He chuckled ever so slightly at that idea.

"I ... I don't know." The effects of the acid quickly compounded, making the room pulsate.

"I've been up all night now."

"You don't have to wait for me."

"You know I can't do that."

"But why?"

"Because I can't," he said, annoyed by the question. Then he got up and went upstairs, while Cholo wagged his tail, looking at me, ready to do the same.

WHAT IS THAT, VELVET?

The antique carousel twirled, but the carnivalesque music was missing the laughter that usually accompanied it. The restored attraction was the centerpiece of Syracuse's Carousel Mall, one of the nation's largest temples of consumerism. At 10 a.m. on a weekday, however, it was dead.

I used to spend my Saturdays here for hours on end. Not to shop, but to meet girls. In my pocket? A pen and index card to collect phone numbers. That was a few years ago, though, and I was no longer a clean-cut kid in Z. Cavaricci jeans. My hair had grown unwieldy, and my flannel shirts were fraying at the sleeves. But that's why I was there.

Samantha had left for Jersey days ago and had not yet returned. I needed to switch things up, especially if she got wind of Reynold's bullshit. I had about two hundred and fifty dollars to my name. I wasn't sure how Shai and I were doing in terms of profitability, but I was very aware we owed Sabs and probably shouldn't be buying anything. But it couldn't hurt to look.

I was headed to Structure, the most expensive men's store I knew, when I recognized a girl working at The Original Cookie

Company. I met Allison at this very same mall three years prior, when I first came here with The Crew. I was trying to show off my skills, especially to Shayan, who called bullshit when I said I batted over .500 in getting digits. I thought back on that day.

"No fucking way, yo," I recalled Shai saying as we took an escalator to a lower level.

"I'm telling you, I'm a good-looking guy." Why wouldn't he take my word for it?

"Says who? Your mom?"

"No, your mom."

"Come on. I'm better looking than you," Shai argued.

"Are you crazy?" I insisted. "Watch and learn today, son."

"Shhhh!" Will and Ryan intervened. Their eyes were looking behind us, as three girls, including Allison, got on the escalator. This was my shot to prove myself.

I introduced myself and asked Allison what school she went to. And she happily responded. We reached the lower floor and someone tugged on my leg, holding me back. I turned around expecting to see one of the guys messing with me. Instead, I found that my shoelace was stuck at the bottom of the escalator. I couldn't move. I looked up at the girls, who were giggling. The Crew was laughing even harder. Despite the embarrassment, I got Allison's number. But she turned out to be a drama queen who called my house several times a day, causing my mom to imagine all sorts of situations until she eventually got the hint and stopped calling.

But now here was Allison again, and I wanted to say hi. She reminded me of a much different time in my life, like five feet of nostalgia wrapped in Levi's and Bath & Body Works Country Apple body spray. I expected Allison to be happy to see me. She couldn't possibly still be mad I never returned her calls. However, when I tried to get her attention, she seemed annoyed, like I was a random dude hitting on her. With my long hair and scruffy face, she had no idea who I was. And she didn't care to find out.

I got to Structure, where I saw a beautiful hunter green and blue plaid flannel. I took it off the rack and held it up. I rubbed my fingers against the material, much higher in quality than the Sears brand my mom bought. It was perfect, but at fifty dollars, it would be the most expensive piece of clothing I'd ever owned. I thought of Allison and how she didn't even recognize the guy she'd stalked for a month. I imagined wearing it on a date with Sam. Well, I could at least try it on.

On my way to the bus stop—Structure bag in hand—I was anxious to connect with Shai to see how on track we were with Johnny's loot. Near the exit, a Jelly Belly gumball machine in a store window caught my eye. Samantha would have loved it, but the price was too steep. No more spending money, I told myself. Then I saw the hair salon.

***

My dad was doing paperwork at the dining room table when I walked in with freshly cropped hair. He smiled— probably in shock—and got up to take a closer look.

He knew me well enough to know he should keep quiet and take the win. But he had questions.

"Who's the girl?"

My dad and I rarely spoke about these sorts of things, but it was obvious he saw an opportunity to bond over whatever broad got me to do what he had begged me to do for two years. I avoided the question and was making my way upstairs when my beeper went off.

"That her?"

I rolled my eyes. It was Shayan, and he paged me "911." This couldn't be good.

Shai was sitting on his bed smoking when I arrived. He was so nervous he didn't even notice I'd chopped off my hair. He laid it all out: He had very little money or weed left and was hoping the same wasn't true for me. But his worries were not unfounded. We had about four hundred dollars between us—half of what we owed Johnny Sabs—and not much product left. Neither of us knew how the hell this happened, yet we both knew exactly how it fucking happened. We smoked and spent it.

We still had a few days to pay Johnny back, which I was hoping was enough to figure something out. Shai asked what we were going to do, as if I had all the answers.

"I don't know what to say to that fat fuck," I replied.

"No. Polish. He's going to be here any minute. Said Johnny wanted him to pick up early."

Oh fuck. "Did you flip that sheet of acid to Paulie?" I asked, hoping that those profits would help bridge the gap.

"Not yet, but look." Shai held a bag with a few pieces of blotter paper in it. Each dose had a red heart on it, not the word "magic" like what we took at the quarry.

"What the fuck is this? This isn't what we tried."

"I know. This is." Shai showed me a baggie with the two last magic doses in it. But that's not what Benji sold us.

A knock on the door caused us to jolt, and we braced ourselves, expecting Polish. But it was Erin from Miami, holding a pack of smokes and a lighter. She let herself right in instead of taking our not-so-subtle hints to get the fuck out. Moments after she sat down and made herself comfortable, there was another knock on the door.

When Polish walked in, it was like watching a WWF wrestler perform ballet at the Met. He was wearing a bright blue Ralph Lauren windbreaker and carrying a "Syracuse University Dad" duffle bag. After a quick "Sup?" he saw Erin sitting on a bean bag doing a crossword puzzle. He looked down at her curiously until she sensed his gaze and smiled. Then he turned back to us.

"I'm sayin', where the good-lookin' girls at?" he asked, right in front of Erin. Before a mortified Shai and I had a chance to apologize, she got up and walked out. Now, Polish had our undivided attention.

"Aight, lemme get the loot," he commanded. But our faces said everything he needed to know.

"How much you short?"

We told Polish the number, and he grimaced. He looked more disappointed than violent, which was somewhat of a relief. I quickly interjected that we'd have that number down to a few hundred in a couple hours, knowing we'd be selling the acid to Paulie. He relaxed a little and gave it some thought.

"Aight, hold up," he said, picking up the phone. "I gotta beep Johnny."

Less than a minute later, that page was returned, and Polish picked up the phone, telling us to wait in the hallway.

That wait was torture. Students went about their day. A couple of people said hi. I looked down to Samantha's room, knowing she was still out of town. A minute went by before Polish knocked from the inside—our cue to go back and learn our fate. There was a long, tense moment while he stared us down. Then, Polish tossed the duffle on Shai's bed. "That's a pound." We were confused.

"A pound, but that's …"

"Double what he gave your sorry asses before, I know. You'll pay him in two weeks."

There was no way we'd be able to move that much that fast. Of course, neither of us said that. We just nodded gratefully.

"I don't need to tell you what will happen if you come up short next time." Then he turned to me. "The fuck happened to your hair?"

"I cut it."

"Yeah, I know." He wanted to kill me for having the stupidity to answer that question.

"By the way, the price has gone up. It's 2 G's. See you soon."

As Polish made his way out, he bumped into Shai's roommate Tyler, who was fumbling with the lock to come in. Polish put his fist up, playfully gesturing like he was going to hit him, causing Tyler to jump. Polish chuckled, "Pussy," as he left the room.

"What just happened?" Shai asked.

"Either we got thrown a lifeline or we're seriously fucked."

The two of us stood there. Our pulses slowed to a normal beat. Tyler put on headphones and opened a textbook.

"That reminds me, I gotta tell you something."

I sat on the bed and listened in disbelief as Shai explained that Reynolds was telling everyone that I confided in him that I had sex with Samantha. And the rumor was spreading like wildfire. "Well, is it true?" Shai asked.

"Don't you think you'd be the first to know if I had sex with Samantha? I haven't even kissed her except that one time."

She's gonna be pissed," I said.

Shai thought long and hard before responding with, "Yeah, probably."

* * *

Four days had passed since Samantha left for New Jersey, and there was still no word from her. I was worried she knew about the rumor. I tried to block out the whole situation, but between that and the Johnny Sabs thing, it was even harder than usual to focus. After wasting all morning in the practice room—I kept my pants on this time—I actually showed up at my drum lesson. It was the first time in a month.

I may have been a decent drummer by teenage rock & roll standards, but the book of rudiments in front of me might as well have been an oral test in Chinese. We were more than halfway through the semester, and I hadn't even opened the book yet, let alone knew how to read the notation. My professor, a guy in his thirties who probably did more drugs than me, leaned back in his chair, watching me struggle. After correcting the way I sat in my chair, he urged me to play the exercise as written.

It took all of five seconds for the professor to adjust the way I held my sticks. Apparently, I didn't even know how to do that. And after stumbling my way across the page at an embarrassingly slow tempo, he corrected my many errors and asked me to take it again from the top. We went through this routine about four or five times. To the professor's credit, he tried to brush it off like it wasn't a big deal. It probably wasn't the first time he'd seen such an unprepared student.

"Let's call it a wrap," he said, more embarrassed for me than I was for myself.

"I'm sorry. I'll practice harder," I said while gathering my things. We both knew that was a lie.

Exiting the room, I exhaled a sigh of relief and noticed a missed page from an area code I didn't recognize. I thought maybe, just maybe, it was Samantha calling from home. But there was no way of calling long distance from OCC. Then I had an idea: the World Wide Web.

I'd never actually used the internet, but I watched Stapes and Craig check Phish setlists and read about the *Thriller* rumor. I was good with computers, having used Robbie's Commodore 64 and the various display models at Sears, and was sure I could figure this out. Entering the OCC library for the first time, I asked a staff member if they had an internet computer and was directed to the one lonely workstation that had the ability to get online.

"But good luck figuring it out," she said. "I don't know how to work that thing."

She wasn't kidding. After twenty minutes, I gave up, blew off the rest of the day, and took the two-hour bus ride home to find out who paged me. As I dialed, I thought of my Jill Campbell experience—I hoped Sam's father didn't answer. Shit, what if it was Luke? I thought about hanging up, but too late—she picked up. There was a brief pause until Samantha spoke. It took me a moment to realize it was her answering machine.

I was relieved it was actually she who called, but annoyed she wasn't there. Unable to take the uncertainty of our situation, I showed up at her room that night unannounced, a wrapped box in hand. It was the Jelly Belly machine.

When Samantha opened her door, Kara, Stapes, Petta, and Reynolds were sitting around their coffee table. My presence seemed to spoil the mood because as soon as they saw me, my short hair, new clothes, and the boxed gift, they scrambled to put away the weed and said their goodbyes. Even Kara left, but not before rolling her eyes at me. It was obvious everyone had heard this bullshit lie from Reynolds, and I was prepared to find one very angry Samantha.

"Hey you!" she said, rubbing my hair. "Oh my gosh, it looks soooo good." If she was pissed about what people were saying, it definitely didn't show. Maybe she didn't know? I tried to prolong any mention of it by handing Samantha the box, and when she unwrapped it to find the Jelly Belly machine, she threw her arms around me. She spoke a mile a minute about how much she missed me before abruptly shifting gears into a serious tone.

"There's this rumor going around," she said. It seemed we were going to have a talk after all.

"I never said whatever it is you heard," I blurted out.

"I know," was all she said before going into a diatribe about how much she missed me, and how she couldn't wait to get back. That she was breaking up with Luke, but not yet, and that she wanted to keep "hanging out," but we had to be careful. It sounded like her mouth wasn't keeping up with her brain, so I kissed her. We were making out when the door swung open. Kara was back.

"I forgot my—" She saw Sam and I embracing and looked annoyed. "ID."

We all stood there for a moment.

"Actually," Kara continued, "I don't feel like going out."

TAKE A BITE OUT OF CRIME

Now that my mind was at ease with Sam, I felt good for the first time in a while. Then I remembered that we had ten days to pay back Johnny Sabs. I told my parents I was staying home sick, and once they left for work, I went to Shai's. Exiting the elevator, it was immediately obvious something was off. Furniture was toppled over, and cuss words were written on some of the whiteboards. When I saw that the one affixed to Sam and Kara's door read "skinny bitches," I knew it was the work of Tammy.

Shai and Tammy were technically still together—she was a junior at Nottingham—though his eyes and other body parts were often elsewhere. She was not excited about the new girls he was hanging out with, and when she showed up unannounced at 6 a.m. to find him not yet home, she went full-on chicken head, vandalizing the hallway and waking up the whole floor by screaming, "Shayan, I'm going to get my abortion now!"

"She's pregnant?" I asked.

"Apparently," he replied nonchalantly, and after a few moments added, "She's fucking crazy. I blacked out at a DU party last night."

Tammy's situation didn't seem to be registering to Shai. He was far more concerned with Johnny Sabs, especially, as he was now telling me, that the acid we sold Paulie turned out to be fake. The wannabe mobster was claiming his clients in Albany were Hell's Angels ready to track us down if they didn't get their money back. I was sure that he was lying about having ties to the infamously violent motorcycle gang, but Shai thought there might some truth to it. In either case, there wasn't much we could do. We didn't have the money.

Shai considered going to Jeremiah and doing whatever it took—violently if necessary—to make Paulie whole. I tried to convince him that Paulie was driving a wedge between us and anyone from our town who would have our back if shit went down. Besides, we already had Johnny Sabs to deal with, who cared about some Hells Angels that probably didn't even exist? There was only one way to sort this all out and come up with a plan: take those last two "magic" doses and strategize.

Popping LSD at 9 a.m. gave us the entire day to stroll around campus, where it really felt like fall. The air was crisp, the leaves showed their colors, and a fading orange sun provided the ivy-covered buildings with a gilded glow. Shai made some small talk, like explaining how the SU basketball team was poised to perform this season, or how he fronted a quarter pound of weed to Lamar. "What, what?!" I was pissed.

Lamar lived in Brewster-Bowland, a dorm otherwise known as "BB." The thing I had recently come to understand was that SU unabashedly segregated each freshman class by socioeconomic status. The kids on The Mount were le creme-de-la-creme. At the other end of the spectrum was BB, which housed mostly scholarship students. The complex was located right outside one of the city's worst areas, right next to a highway that ran through the city and separated the have-nots from the take-what-you-haves. It was the only dorm with twenty-four-seven security.

Shai explained that while business had slowed on The Mount, BB was still dry. I knew that the first harvest of kind bud had arrived because someone in Flint had brought back a couple ounces from NYC. But Shai was sure that wouldn't be an issue at BB. No one there even knew what the hell kind bud was. Most importantly, he said, Lamar was trustworthy.

"Why didn't you talk to me first?" I asked. Fronting someone, let alone someone we didn't really know, was a bad idea. I mean, look at the situation we were already in.

"'Cause I knew you wouldn't be okay with it. Anyway, I'm not the one who bought new clothes, a fancy haircut, and a gift for a girl I aint' even banging." That was low, and Shai was quick to apologize.

"Just so you know, the haircut was nine bucks."

"You got ripped off, homie."

As we continued our walk around campus, leaves swirling in psychedelic formations, we arrived at the Shine Student Center. It seemed to be pretty happening for such an early hour, so we went inside to check out what was going on. Small crowds congregated around various wall-mounted televisions, and we remembered that the OJ Simpson verdict was that day. We weren't going to miss this historic event, and as we struggled to get a good view of proceedings, Shai said he knew a spot in the basement that usually had big screens set up for football games.

He was right. We went through a long, concrete stairway that in our state felt like a rabbit hole, arriving at a large assembly room where students were gathered around a huge screen. The place was packed, but somehow, we managed to find two seats near the back. It was perfect.

"How do you know about this place?" I asked.

"I have no fucking clue."

While we stared at the broadcast, waiting for the judge to enter the courtroom, I glanced around the room. At first, I saw a few black students, and then a few more. Actually, every person in here, except for me and Shai, was black. It seemed to hit both of us at the same time: We were watching the OJ verdict with the African-American Student Union, and if he was found guilty, it wouldn't be wise to be the only white dudes around. And as the jury clerk read the verdict, the tension grew stronger and stronger, magnified by the strong acid.

"We the jury in the above-entitled action find the defendant, Orenthal James Simpson …"

Buckle up, here we go.

And waiting.

Still waiting.

"… not guilty of the crime of murder …"

"WOO HOO!!!!!!!!!!!!!!!!!!!!!!!!"

The place erupted in hugs and high fives. I saw one person cry. But I don't think anyone in that room was as relieved as us. We would live to see another day. Anything after that, however, was still up in the air. The next day, Shai gave Paulie half of his money back. His rationale was that he had to see the dude every day, unlike Johnny who he could hide from. That, however, was not so easy for me.

* * *

In a matter of forty-eight hours, the cute autumn nip in the air turned into a twenty-four-seven slap in the face. It was even worse on Onondaga Hill, where the wind would enter your throat and suck the oxygen out of you. The notion of smoking cigarettes all day outside the student center was no longer appealing. So, when I ran into Jake McCallistair, who asked if I wanted to hang in his car, that sounded great.

When I pulled a bag of weed out, Jake instantly stopped me. "Harvest is here," were his only words as he took a hand-blown glass jar out of his glove compartment. He pulled off the cork stopper and let me smell the lush, green, moist bud inside. This was the one and only kind bud, and it got us high as all hell. As we sat there, Jake put in a Phish tape—last year's Halloween show—and expressed how badly he wanted to be in Chicago when they played *Thriller*.

I rolled my eyes. Then I got an idea.

"Can you get more of this?"

"Does Jim Boeheim play a mean zone defense? Fuck yeah, I can get more of this."

I hopped out of the car with a plan to help pay Johnny Sabs back. The enthusiasm must have gone to my head because for whatever reason, I went to my music history class for the first time in weeks. I arrived unsure if I was in the right room. The room looked different. Larger. Then it occurred to me that it was not the space that had changed, but the number of people in it. The professor was right: Most people had dropped the class by now. More importantly, however, was that those who remained had nothing on their desks but #2 pencils. Midterms. Shit.

I stared at the blank Scantron sheet with disdain, taunting me. The questions on the exam made little sense. The chance I would get more than three of the fifty of them right was about as likely as my being able to belt out a violin concerto. It was a debacle. I guessed nearly every answer and headed for the two-hour bus ride to SU via a transfer downtown.

While I waited at the bus stop, angry that I was once again failing in school, I had a smoke with one of the student center stoners. He informed me that If I dropped my classes before the end of the semester, I could get withdrawals on my transcript instead of F's. It would be like the whole thing never happened, and I could pull myself together next January. I made a mental note to formally withdraw, right next to "Don't get shot by Johnny Sabs."

My first stop on campus was to see Samantha, but she wasn't home. It was Kara who came to the door, looking like she hadn't slept in a couple days. She had no clue where Samantha was, only that she was out with Reynolds last night.

"What does that mean?" I asked.

She stared at me for a moment, a long moment, and then let out, "Looks like your novelty wore off," before closing the door in my face.

Over at Shai's, I found out Samantha wasn't the only one MIA. Lamar hadn't been returning his calls. We were a week into our deadline, so I brought up the idea of using our remaining funds to buy two ounces of kind bud from Mcallistair and sell them for double what they would normally go for. Shai didn't like the idea, but I informed him it was too late. I'd already made the deal.

"Why didn't you ask me?" he asked.

"Because I knew you'd say no."

There was a moment while we stood there, unsure of how to proceed, and, perhaps, resigned to our fate.

"Yo, you ever do coke?" he asked out of nowhere.

It was an odd thing to ask. No one in The Crew had done it, and Shai knew I only liked drugs that made me think—something I was pretty sure coke didn't make you do. But why the question? After I pressed for more info, he told me that Reynolds had a friend in town from NYU who brought up some blow. Samantha, Erin, and Reynolds did a bunch the other night. Guess that wasn't weed they were so quick to put away when I showed up.

"The last thing I need is a coke head business partner," I joked. Shai chuckled.

"Yeah, well," he said. "I think after you sell that kind bud and we find Lamar, we should close shop."

"Uh, yeah, I know."

* * *

The way those two ounces of kind bud sold reminded me of the Cabbage Patch Kids in the 80's. Before I even had the weed in hand, Shai told Stapes who informed God knows who, and my pager was beeping non-stop. I sold to pampered Long Island chicks, lacrosse players, preppy New England types, the daughter of a very famous CEO, The Mount's official hippies-in-residence Mitch, Sean, and Corey, and, of course, Lior. Within a day, I sold all but three bags, which I planned to unload the next day. With over fifteen hundred dollars in hand, I went to tell Shai that we were good, as long as Lamar came through with at least some money. We had a full week to spare.

Before going home, I gave Samantha's room one more try, but no one was there. I began the walk home when a familiar number appeared on my pager. It was Seth, the hemp-necklace-wearing, green goatee kid across the hall from Lior. I turned around and headed his way.

The smell of incense and sounds of Jimi Hendrix filled Seth's room. The only light came from two lava lamps that gave a nearby Alice in Wonderland-inspired black light poster a trippy purple glow. Seth was playing the guitar on his bed and didn't hear me knock or enter, but his face lit up when he saw I was there. Putting down the guitar, he got up and gave me a hug. Then he handed me an envelope that looked too thin to contain cash. Seth stood there with a big smirk on his face as I opened it, puzzled, to find no money inside. But there was something much more valuable, at least to me: four orange and black hologram-printed mail order tickets for Phish's Halloween show in Chicago. I wanted to jump in the air in jubilation but quickly came back down to Earth. Phish tickets weren't going to keep Johnny Sabs from fucking us up.

"I'm sorry, man, I can't," I told a very disappointed Seth. "Just cash."

Seth complained that his parents only gave him a few grand to last until Thanksgiving, but he had already spent it all and was living off his meal plan for the next month. He had purchased the tickets months ago for his high school friends, but they were all scattered around at different colleges, and none were up for a trip to Chicago. He asked a second time if I'd be willing to make the trade, which I almost was. But my better judgment said get the hell out of that room before I did something stupid.

Walking from Seth's room to the elevator, the thought of what I was passing up nagged me. Four tickets meant not only that Craig and I would be able to go, but we could offer a ticket or two to someone in exchange for a ride—like I did for Woodstock, only for real. I imagined kicking myself in a couple years for not going to what I knew would be a historic show. Visualizing being in that arena on acid, I longed for that feeling of bouncing around the room. I moved mountains to make it to Woodstock, and now all that was in front of me was a hill. But it was a hill with Johnny Sabs on the other side. Possibly with a gun.

Less than two minutes later, I was back in Seth's room making the trade. Four tickets for three eighths. In other words, we would be three hundred and seventy dollars short for Johnny Sabs. Possibly more if Lamar didn't turn up.

"I'm jealous," Seth said.

"Why?"

"You're seeing Thriller."

KNOWING IS HALF THE BATTLE

The snowfall on this dark evening was heavy and accumulating fast. As I snuck out of my house, careful not to wake my parents, I left the porch and rounded the corner to wait for my ride. It was around eleven, and the only sound was my feet pressing into the soft snow. As I waited, I looked down at my insufficiently warm mustard-yellow coat. Nearly a year after the Madison Square Garden incident, my mom was still mad I lost my Starter jacket, and this was her replacement. This thing almost stood out more than my Dolphins gear.

I didn't even ask my parents about going to Chicago, so I left a note. I imagined how mad Shai would be when he discovered I'd spent our money just days before we needed to pay Johnny. It was a shitty thing to do, but I needed to get away. The past few weeks were some of the most intense in my life, and what better place to get it all out than at a Phish show? And not any show, but *Halloween*. I smiled to myself, excited this was actually happening, as a small car—seemingly too feeble to navigate this weather—turned the corner and pulled over. Jake McCallistair, in his ancient Escort, rolled down his window.

"Thriller, buddy. Let's do it!"

A dog barked in the distance, no doubt waking someone up. Glad it wasn't Cholo. As I got in the car and said hi to Craig, "Beat It" was in the tape deck. I turned to Petta, who came along to see firsthand what this thing was all about—why his friends were willfully becoming, in his mind, losers all for the sake of a band. Together, we began the ten-hour overnight journey to the windy city.

The drive was filled with good conversation and Craig's never-ending stash of weed. Along the way, I eagerly explained to Petta that being on LSD was an integral part of the experience. Only while tripping would one actually understand how mind-bending and exhilarating a Phish show could be. Only on acid was it possible to truly "bounce around the room." Craig was always skeptical about this. He never did psychedelics and didn't think they really enhanced the music.

It saddened me that Craig willfully missed out on what I considered to be the only way to see the band we loved. To me, acid and Phish went hand in hand. Petta, on the other hand, bought my spiel, happily agreeing to find doses as soon as we hit the Rosemont Horizon parking lot.

Winter came early in Chicago, and it was freezing. A warm, one-dollar, garlic grilled cheese sandwich provided temporary comfort while Petta and I went on our mission for acid. It didn't take long. Within minutes, we found pyramid-branded blotter paper. We each popped two, timing it to kick in right before showtime. An hour later, we were already tripping hard, looking around the sold-out arena, which was packed with anxious energy for the evening to come.

"Look at all these people," Petta said, his voice wavering with a slight psychedelic twinge. "How many of them do you think are tripping their balls off?"

I looked around. The arena was bright. A cloud of smoke from the hundreds of pipes, joints, and cigarettes being smoked floated above the stage like a cloud. The black and orange seats, coincidentally apropos of the holiday, glowed.

"The chairs look like Arkanoid," said Petta. Clearly the acid had kicked in.

"I'm really glad you decided to, you know, partake tonight," I responded. "You're really gonna get the full experience." But Petta was in his own world. "These people are all hooked. It's insane."

I thought about it; he had a point. I mean, here I was in the middle of Chicago on a freezing night, on drugs with barely enough money for food, and all to see this band perform as if my life depended on it.

"I know," was all I was able to say. The doses were hitting hard now.

There was a long pause.

"How are we talking right now?" Petta asked.

It was a good question. I didn't remember ever opening my mouth. And Petta wasn't moving his either. Were we communicating telepathically? Suddenly, the arena went black, and the crowd roared as the band took the stage. The first thing I noticed was that Trey cut his hair. The scruffy frontman of the band, who always had long hair like my own, had cut it short—just like I did. That was weird.

Why does this have to be so fucking weird? I thought.

Petta turned to me, concerned. "This is weird," he said. The two of us were on the exact same page. Craig, meanwhile, sparked up yet another bowl.

"*Welcome,*" Phish frontman Trey Anastasio said to the crowd, as the band members let out deep, sinister laughs that echoed throughout the arena. Something was off. I was still a newbie to Phish, but it was common knowledge that the band almost never directly addressed the audience. "*We just want to get things started off right tonight, so before we get rolling, I just want to make everyone knows what they need to do to keep in tune with the whole thing here tonight.*" Trey was saying what I'd known all along—that you needed to be on acid to understand what was really happening at a show. "*We don't want anyone to do anything too weird or scary; things tend to get weird when we're around.*"

Petta and I stared at one another. What the fuck was happening? Trey came out and admitted—no, confessed!—to everything we were talking about. I looked at Craig and Mcallistair. They didn't see anything other than a normal Phish show, and most of the audience seemed oblivious too. But the cheers of a handful of others told us we weren't the only ones in tune—or attuned—with the band tonight.

Trey continued, "*I hope everyone is planning to follow what's written in a very special book. It's such a great book. It's a deep and meaningful book. It's a powerful book. The book has saved me so many times in the past, and when things get weird later on, I'm sure the book will save you ..."*

Special book? What was he talking about, the Torah? Petta was as confused as me. And how was it possible that Craig and Jake, standing there with stoned silly grins, were oblivious to what Trey was really talking about? Was it really because they weren't on acid? Then Trey's tone and demeanor quickly changed.

"Wait a minute. I don't think it's going to work tonight. It's too weird. I feel too many evil Halloween spirits in the air!"

The emotions of the past couple months boiled inside me—joy, anger, and ecstasy overcame me all at once. Since I first visited The Mount, I'd been exposed to new types of people, of thinking, and of life that had brought passion, confusion, and violence into my world. Samantha. Reynolds. Johnny Sabs. Cocaine. The Spot. It was a psychological and soulful reckoning.

"The book can't take it! The book is getting its ass kicked! But if you read the book, it's kind of a battle between the book and the evil spirits." Trey no longer seemed like the nerdy, peace and love icon he was. He looked angry, militant, and possessed. At this moment, he transformed into Zach De La Rocha from Rage Against the Machine.

Book. Spirits. Book spirit, fuck spirits! AAAHHHH!!!!!

This was the ultimate moment of catharsis, as I let out a battle cry. Not just against what I'd experienced the past few weeks, but everything that had been holding me back my entire life.

The last few lines of the song conveyed that we, the attuned, had deliberately been led to this very moment by the band.

A cold and lonely night.

Running the pace of her fright.

And now that we knew the band had lured us here, Trey let us know, with the song's final words, that we were about to find out how and why.

Look in the face tonight!

And with that, the opening chords of "Divided Sky" set the night in motion. The instrumental song sounded more majestic than ever. As the band delved into the twisted "Mary Had a Little Lamb" segment of the song—a palindrome pattern that is played and then repeated backward—everything in my field of vision froze, and the orange and black seats morphed into an icon that I'd seen many times before. The graphic was so familiar that its meaning was understood even without those words that traditionally accompanied it: "Your regularly scheduled programming is being interrupted."

Suddenly it felt like I was ushered through a set of doors and that the attention of the entire audience was on me. I had seen this, too, before: the proud applause of a studio audience watching someone experience the profound. It was the set of *This is Your Life*. And that someone was me.

My trance was broken by Petta handing me a small, metal object. It was Craig's packed bowl. But in my state, I couldn't figure out what it was.

"What is it?" I asked.

Petta looked at me with an intense stare and voiced three words that sent a chill through my spine. "It's the bait."

He was right. *This* was what got me into Phish. *This* was why I was failing out of school. *This* was why I was in another part of the country, with people I barely knew, for another fix of that euphoric sensation I first encountered while hearing "*Bouncing Around the Room.*" I had been duped, and I was infuriated.

I accepted the pipe from Petta and launched it far into the crowd, before turning my attention back to the stage. A moment later, Craig asked Petta where the bowl was.

"E.R. threw it."

That's when things went downhill fast.

* * *

When the last notes of *Divided Sky* reverberated around the arena, Trey let out a two-note motif that I'd heard before. It was "Wilson"—the Gamehendge saga song they opened up with at MSG the night I went to the hospital. This time I knew the song all too well, but the lyrics took on a much different meaning. Wilson was not some fictional character. He was not even a person at all. Wilson was a metaphor for everything that had been standing in my way. Unlike at MSG, when I didn't know what or why people were chanting, I joined angrily against ignorance, stupidity, and *the bait*.

Gamehenge was real. Gamehendge was us. Gamehendge was now.

Wiiiiiilllllson!

Wiiiiiilllllson!

I now grasped how dire my situation was. My life was heading nowhere. I was stoned every waking hour of the day. This was not unnoticed by Phish, whose line, *"Now you got me back thinking* that you're the worst one. *I must inquire, Wilson, can you still have fun?"* resonated like gospel. I was overcome with emotion, nearly brought to my knees when Trey morphed into Zach De La Rocha again. He shouted into the mic, with a thumb and index finger extended in the form of a gun, his voice as poised and angry as a gangster rapper:

BOP BOOM BA BIGGY BOOM BOOM BOOM!

After a massive guitar solo, Wilson ended, and a more lighthearted "Ya Mar" eased the tension. But its words were no less meaningful. The line, *"Don't ask them what it was. Tell them what it is,"* made me think of The Spot and how I knew better than the slimeballs who went there or to Harry's. It also made me think of *Thriller*. Again, I knew better. I needed to be confident in my abilities. *"Now you look so good, I want to love you dead,"* brought to mind the girl with whom I had become obsessed.

I turned to Petta and said, "Samantha," thinking he would understand, but he looked confused. I thought everyone knew there was something between us, but I guess he hadn't heard. But as a beam of white light hovered over Petta's head, I now understood that he was guiding me through this life altering experience, like the ghost of Christmas past from *Scrooged* or a guardian spirit from *It's a Wonderful Life*.

"Are you an angel?" I asked, but as the band played a new song—another one from that night at MSG, called "Sparkle"— our voices became inaudible through the sounds.

The pressure builds when you buy a gift, you're hoping that your dread will lift. It glitters on her like a glass. You shudder as it comes to pass.

I thought of the Jelly Belly Machine. Then the people I'd met in Flint and Day halls. The Mount was less than a mile from Westcott, but it was a universe apart.

Your friends confine you in their worlds.
One by one, a string of pearls.
Confused you say, this isn't me.
You hover in their unity.
Ashamed, you slowly lose your grasp.
Release the links, undo the clasp.

As these words "*laugh and laughing fall apart*" were repeated over and over as the tempo increased to a near impossible pace, I was losing any remaining semblance of reality. Rosemont Horizon spun around and around until the song abruptly ended. And with one gigantic rocking chord, the band brought us into the triumphant sonic landscape of a new song called "Free."

"It feels like we're swimming," Petta said, speaking for the first time since handing me the bait. The lights were aquatic, and our bodies swayed like treading in the ocean. Finally, I felt what I experienced at SPAC. The weightlessness of "*Bouncing Around the Room*," only intensified a thousand times. And as the aggressive chords quieted down, the lights dimmed, and Trey sang the first verse in a now intensely quiet arena, I was illuminated by a spotlight and that all eyes were on me. This was *MY* life.

I'm floating in the blimp a lot,
I feel the feeling I forgot,
of swimming weightless in the womb,
WHILE BOUNCING GENTLY ROUND THE ROOM.
In a minute I'll be free,

and we'll be splashing in the sea.
I feel no curiosity,
I see the path ahead of me.
In a minute I'll be free and you'll be splashing in sea,
we hear a tiny cry as we go sliding by.
Free!!!!!!

The lyric's reference to "Bouncing Around the Room" was an obvious admission that I, like many others, had been lured there that night. As I danced, the music vibrated through my bones. It was this dancing that connected all of us. It was this dancing that put us in the trance-like state that forced us to abandon all sense of responsibility to get here. And the reason we were here? It was a grand effort to change our lives.

It was now clear why I had almost failed every grade. It was because I didn't see the world as a real place. But I now grasped that it was a living and breathing ecosystem with real ramifications for its five billion people, including myself. And the main culprit of my intellectual blindness—as with my entire generation—was a lifelong barrage of mind-numbing media. Corporations like MTV had taught us to worship vanity. But now, free of its grasp, those attuned were undergoing a metamorphosis.

During the song's lengthy jam section, the realization that I was about to withdraw from my first semester as a percussion major in community college sunk in. Then Trey picked up a pair of drumsticks and banged away on a small upright mini kit set up next to him—this was new to me—while the rest of the band played harsh and dissonant chords that sounded as if they were being amplified through a jet propeller. The lights were no less sinister, with dark hues and smoke machines making the entire scene feel less like a fish tank and more like hell. Then I got why this was happening. It was a drum circle like the one in Saratoga.

Thinking I was supposed to take part in this transformative session, I banged on seats around me, causing many people to look on in concern. As Trey, and I, continued, it was revealed this wasn't only about personal change. This was the awakening of a movement to change the world.

The next song—yet another I didn't know—explained two things: the science behind how we'd been kept in the dark our whole lives by the major media conglomerates, and how Phish was able to use those same techniques to bring us here. It was a hypnotization technique called "Guyute" that left us in an addiction-like state, fiending for another fix.

Guyute was the ugly pig
who walked on me and danced a jig
that he had learned when he was six,
then stopped and did some other tricks,
like pulling weapons from his coat
and holding them against my throat,
he lectured me in a language strange
and scampered quickly out of range.

The song, which began with an Irish folk feel to, quickly turned into anxiety-filled, techno-like trance music. Its repetitive beats and electronic pulsations made me think of the mom at the NYC hospital who spoke of the effects of rap. About a minute into this, the speed increased to a frenzy and the light show made the Rosemont Horizon glow a deep red reminiscent of an inferno.

It was now obvious that the band had programmed us over months just to deprogram us tonight. The point? To illustrate how Guyute works and help us understand who we are, where we needed to be, and how to get there. This was all answered with a vision of fulfilling my dream of being in the film business, not only to make movies but create meaningful content that would counter the effects of crappy pop culture. My life now had a purpose.

As the eerie techno section of the song built to a furious climax, Fishman, the drummer, executed a glorious break that erupted into a transcendent melody. It was reminiscent of the dramatic orchestral music during emotional reveals on *This is Your Life*. In the blink of an eye, the lights dimmed, the smoke cleared, and the deafening roar of the crowd hushed to a silence in which you could hear a pin drop. But the song was not yet over, as Trey stepped up to the mic to explain the method behind all of this.

I'm bouncing like a newborn elf.
I can't remain inside myself.
Guyute glances in my eyes,
AND MANAGES TO HYPNOTIZE.
As I sleep the sleep of death,
he sucks from me my only breath
that I had breathed since I was ten.

The science of Guyute goes all the way back to birth, when we became inundated with messages constructed by the mass media to keep us from fulfilling our spiritual potential. The band used similar tactics—music accentuated by drugs—to throw our lives away in pursuit of that next dose. And the song's last line conveyed it perfectly:

I HOPE THIS HAPPENS ONCE AGAIN!

* * *

"Run Like an Antelope" was one of my favorite tunes and almost always a set closer. That was a relief because by this point, my mind was in desperate need of a break. Mostly instrumental and improvisational, there were few lyrics, with the only line of substance being:

"*Set the gearshift for the high gear of your soul. You've got to run like an antelope out of control.*"

At this point, I recalled the Land of Oz. It certainly was not the first acid trip to take on elements of that cinematic classic, nor the last, but for me it wasn't the 1940's masterpiece of which I thought. It was *The Wiz*. And when "You've got to run like an antelope out of control!" was repeated over and over, what I had actually heard was *you've got to ease on down, ease on down the road*. I was yelling this in random people's faces, shoving a young kid who was with his mother. But the song ended before things could get worse. There was a brief break after the song, which everyone assumed signaled the end of the set. And while people were heading to the bathrooms, the lights hadn't come back on, and the band was still on stage. Then the four members all sang in acapella:

"*Oom pah pah, oom pah pah, oom pa pa!*"

At first, I didn't know why Phish sang those words, but then I grasped its similarity to the classic comedic *wah wah wah* sound from Charlie Brown. They had pranked us! As Fishman kicked off a new song with a slow and complex beat in an odd time signature, the rest of the band joined in creepy sounding chords. We the attuned now knew that the past eighteen months had been one big setup. And we all fell for it for hook, line, and sinker.

The lyrics to "Harpua" perfectly described what I had felt since first seeing the dancing "zombies" at SPAC. They explained that while the grimy people on tour—like the girl I got my acid from at MSG—distributed the drugs that plugged us into the scene and made us susceptible to Guyute, they didn't care about us. They didn't care about Phish. They were here for one thing and one thing only: to get innocent kids fucked up on drugs and destroy their lives.

Hot liquor stone jack,
bitter toothless flesh,
shabby pimple chin-slime,
evil milky rash,
me and Harpua,
spastic dead-eyed hound, oozing dreadlock skullcap,
we're coming to your town,
WE'LL HELP YOU PARTY DOWN!
Me and Harpua,
we couldn't care few-a,
it happens all the time.

On that last line, the band played two staccato notes that brought the song to an upbeat pace, indicating something was about to change. And, indeed, Trey stepped up to the mic and yet again directly addressed the crowd.

"*It's Halloween night in Gamehendge,*" he said to a now out-of-control audience. Trey spoke of a boy named Jimmy, who was home at his parents' house snug in his bed. That's exactly where I wished I was. I thought of my dad. Was he angry? Was he worried? How could I let him down? Why did he refuse to see the beauty and deep meaning in Phish's music?

But then the story took on a more serious note, as Trey told us of a killer dog called Harpua who was walking through Jimmy's town. But no one knew of the imminent danger because everyone was asleep.

"*And they're all asleep and having this simultaneous nightmare together. Everyone was dreaming the same dream simultaneously— just as you will all dream this dream when you go home tonight. But one person wasn't dreaming that dream. And that person was Jimmy. Jimmy wasn't dreaming that dream because Jimmy wasn't asleep.*"

Jimmy was a representation of all of us who were attuned that night. I looked at Craig and McCallistair, and the thousands of other people like them in a stoned haze, oblivious to the proselytizing. They were all asleep while others, such as myself, were very awake with eyes wide open. We were all Jimmy.

But none of us were prepared for what Trey was about to say next:

"*Jimmy was sleeping on his couch with his cat Poster Nutbag, playing his favorite album, which was the very same album that Phish was playing as their Halloween album at the Rosemont Horizon that night!*"

The crowd went absolutely wild upon hearing those words. Were they going to don their musical costume now and not wait until the next set? The band answered that unvoiced question by bursting into a familiar song—none other than "Beat It" from Michael Jackson's *Thriller*! What the fuck?! Despite months of this rumor, it was hard to believe this was actually the album they were going to play!

But wait—the band abruptly stopped playing after thirty seconds or so, laughing at this absurdity. It was a joke—a Halloween trick as opposed to a treat. This was their way of saying "Of course we're not playing Thriller, dummies. We were fucking with you this whole time! *We* started the rumor!" After the audience realized they'd been duped and the laughs subsided, *Harpua* resumed. But it was too much, and I was spinning out of control like Dorothy's house in *The Wizard of Oz*. In fact, I now knew why Trey and Mike were talking about dreaming. Like Dorothy in Oz, this was all a dream.

The room was now twirling, and the grip of sheer panic took over me. My clothes were confining; I started to undress. And then suddenly the first set was over, the lights were on, and I stood on top of my chair, in my underwear, clicking my heels together and yelling, "There's no place like home!"

Dozens of people stared as I clicked my heels together a second time. And a third.

"There's no place like home! There's no place like home!"

Boom! Someone put me in a full nelson and dragged me away.

A DOSE OF REALITY

* * *

My limbs were heavy in the cold and deep water, while the sound of familiar voices in the near distance comforted me. I tried swimming towards them but was met with a stiff resistance that brought me back to reality. I wasn't in the ocean; I was in a dingy room tucked away in the Rosemont Horizon, my wrists and ankles shackled to a wall.

"Holy shit," Craig said, observing the chains. He held my yellow jacket in his arms as Petta stood next to him with a vacant, bewildered look in his eyes. While Craig spoke to the security guard watching over me, two EMTs took the shackles off and tied me down to a gurney.

Wham! I was jolted awake as two heavy doors opened up in front of my stretcher, and I was led outside into the freezing cold. I thought back to *Cruis'n USA*, the arcade game they had at Day Hall. For the past few weeks, Stapes, Petta, Craig, and a stocky bearded football player named Vinnie Warner would play it stoned. And every time someone crashed, Warner would yell "Wham!!!!" at the top of his lungs, his deep tenor voice sounding like barbells falling on a gymnasium floor.

Another *wham!* brought me back to the present, where I was being led into an ambulance. Eventually I arrived at a local emergency room, going through yet another set of double doors. I waited, handcuffed to a stretcher, for a room to open up. The staff placed me far from the lobby so I wouldn't cause a scene, but it wasn't far enough. As nurses and doctors went about their work in the quiet and sterile environment, I thought that if I yelled "wham" loud enough, I would snap out of this nightmare and find myself back on Westcott Street—because, you know, there's no place like home.

"Wham!" I screamed, causing two doctors to drop their papers, sheets flying into the air. A nurse hung up the phone and came my way. My plan didn't work; I was still there. I took a deep breath to belt out the loudest mother fucking wham of all time, but another nurse towered over me, needle in hand. I thought of the scene in Quentin Tarantino's *Reservoir Dogs* where a cop is bound to a chair while his tormentor dances to "Stuck in the Middle With You." It was a song Five Layer Burrito covered, and tonight I sang it. Loudly.

As the nurse inched closer, my voice grew stronger, and I sang faster and faster until suddenly there was a needle in my arm.

Stuck in the middle with y—

And I was out.

STRANGER DANGER

On the long ride back from Chicago, Craig helped make sense of the show with the clarity and perspective of someone much more familiar with Phish—and way more sober—than I had been. The opening monologue from Trey, he explained, was actually a rarely played Gamehendge song called "Icculus." Every performance of it featured a different, bizarre narration.

"But all that stuff about it being weird, that's what Petta and I were talking about, right? And then Trey comes out and says exactly that?" I looked to Petta for support, who nodded in agreement.

"It was Halloween," Craig interjected. "What did you expect?"

"What was the deal with Trey's drum kit?" I asked, referencing the set up that caused me to bang on seats, imagining I was part of a larger drum circle.

"It's a new song. And Trey's had those on stage all fall. I read about it on AOL."

I was disappointed. Had the night been nothing more than a total delusion? As Craig continued, I learned that "Guyute" was about a deranged pig of the same, and that the band hadn't played the song in years—that's why the crowd went nuts. And "Harpua," like "Icculus," always contained a narration. In fact, Phish had three such songs. Each one was played infrequently, and they almost never played more than one in the same show.

All of that information would have been very helpful twenty-four hours ago.

I sunk in my seat. I felt like a new person—motivated and determined—but also worried that I had lost my mind. At bare minimum, there had to be a kernel of reality in what I had witnessed. And if the band could transform my mindset so dramatically, imagine the potential for my entire generation. The question was if the band knew they had this power. The answer came in a Eureka moment: I needed to inform the band how influential they could be by writing them a letter and hand delivering it.

Ultimately, however, my primary concerns were Johnny Sabs and Samantha. Overwhelmed by the pressure, I went to grab a smoke out of my pocket and pulled out a pink slip the doctor gave me. A prescription. It simply read: "Do not do LSD or any other hallucinogens ever again." It was good advice. As we passed through Ohio into New York State, I asked what we were listening to.

"*Quadrophenia* by The Who," Craig informed me. "It's the album Phish played last night."

It was pouring rain when Mcallistair dropped us off at Day Hall. Craig had explained everything to Stapes over the phone, so he and the guys were out front waiting. As Stapes gave us a bear hug, I saw Shai. I wondered how pissed he was at me for spending the Sabs money. The two of us hadn't laid hands on each other since there was a drunken incident at Jonah's when we were fifteen, but as he approached, he raised his arm, and I expected a fight. Instead, he embraced me.

"At least you kept your underpants on this time," he said.

"Barely," I managed through a hard laugh I needed badly.

"You aight?"

I took a moment to really think about that. Despite my body feeling like crap, I was exhilarated about what I experienced and everything to come. But how could I even begin to explain it?

"Yo, there's some crazy shit I gotta' tell you." I struggled to find the words. "Phish is more than just a band."

Shai looked slightly concerned. I decided this was not at all the right time to talk about it—if ever. I changed the subject. "Anyway, what I miss?"

"Well, Reynold's gone," he explained, shrugging off any sense of unease. "I guess he went on a three-day coke bender, and his parents pulled him out. He's not coming back."

"Wow, that's crazy."

"Oh, and Tammy's not pregnant. She made that shit up."

I laughed. After all, it was funny. Then I remembered we were in some serious shit.

"And Johnny?" I asked.

There had been no sightings of Sabs while I was gone. But with only a few days left to pay him, it was only a matter of time before he appeared. And once the semester was over, it would be a lot harder to hide. We needed to find Lamar, and fast. Shai told me to get some sleep, and we would deal with it in the morning. But first I wanted to see Samantha.

"Yo, go home, man. Your mom is probably freaking out, and your dad's gonna be pissed."

He was right. I definitely was not looking forward to dealing with all that. But I had to go see her.

"Dude, trust me. You should go home."

"I will."

* * *

I had a speech prepared to give Samantha, essentially an ultimatum to dump Luke or there would be no "us," even though I was in no position to be giving her a choice, nor did I even know what sort of "us" there was. When Sam answered the door, I was relieved she was alone. With Kara gone, I would tell her how I felt.

"Samantha, I need to t—"

"Hey, you," she said, her words of endearment now sounding half-hearted at best, fake at worst, and tinged with nervousness either way. As I spoke, she interrupted—like she didn't want me there. Then I saw why. Coming back from the bathroom was a big dude with long hair. I couldn't tell if he was a hippie or a lumberjack.

"Luke, this is my friend E.R.," she said.

All this time I had an image of what her boyfriend looked like—a classic white hat wearing private school herb. But the reality was he looked a bit like. Well, me, only taller and stronger.

I told Sam I'd see her later and turned around when Luke flashed a big smile.

"Hey man, what's the rush?" he said, pulling a bag of bright and beautiful kind bud from his duffle bag. While I sat down, Luke draped his arm around Samantha in a confrontational way. His heavy laugh was dominated by bass notes as he packed a large hand-blown glass bowl exactly like Craig's three-hundred-dollar one. A few minutes later, the room was smokey and tense. Samantha was clearly uncomfortable. We lit up cigarettes. There was an excruciatingly long pause.

"What's this?" he asked, eyeing the gumball machine. "You always wanted one of those stupid things."

"Luke." Samantha looked sad—and a little scared.

"See, she's still a dork." He got up and examined the machine, shaking it around.

"I like the Jalapeno ones," he said, still shaking the machine, trying to find the exact flavor that suited him.

"I'm gonna get going," I said.

"Hey, I'm sorry, man. Where are my manners?" He extended his arm for a handshake while using his other arm to put the machine back on her desk. But he let go of it a little too forcefully, causing the glass to shatter and land around my feet. I stood there, half in disbelief and half appreciating the symbolic nature of what had happened. Samantha looked at me with sympathetic but helpless eyes as I turned away and left the room.

* * *

Over a week went by without a word from Sam, and our Jonny Sabs deadline had passed. There was nothing left for us to do but hide. As I woke on an uncharacteristically sunny November morning, I pulled myself out of my funk and decided it was time to buckle down: I would officially withdraw from class. But, as I got dressed, my dad barged in my room.

"Did you go to the hospital in Chicago?"

Holy fuck. How did he know?

"Umm, no. Of course not. Why?"

Then he produced a piece of paper. He read it aloud: "Do not take LSD or any other hallucinations ever." I didn't know how to even begin.

"It's a joke, dad. Me and my friends were playing ar—"

"Don't lie to me," he said through clenched teeth. I hadn't seen him that mad in a long time—since Zopie's. But as I stood there, unsure of what to say, his body relaxed. And his posture shifted from irate to defeated. I couldn't blame him. But if he knew what I had seen on Halloween, he would know that things would soon be different. If only I could tell him that my entire outlook on life had changed.

"Dad, I'm done with that crap. I'm getting my shit together."

He smiled, which was a relief, until I saw that he wasn't amused.

"That's what you always say. Why should I believe you now?"

I opened my mouth to explain my mission. About Phish.

About how they had a role to play in creating a better world. But I kept quiet. A few minutes later, he left to make a furniture delivery, and I went to take the bus to the registrar's office.

A DOSE OF REALITY

Waiting at the bus stop in front of my house, I questioned myself. Everything from that bad trip in Chicago was seriously fucking with my head. It didn't feel like a bad trip; it was more like a real memory that lived viscerally in my brain. And while it was very unlikely that Trey actually turned into Zach De La Rocha, I knew one thing for certain—I needed to get my letter to the band.

That letter hadn't yet been written, and I wasn't even sure what it would say. But I planned to type it up on the library's McIntosh as soon as I finished at the registrar's office. I smiled to myself, optimistic. Then a deep purple car came into view, driving my way up Westcott. It was a Mercury Cougar. Johnny Sabs.

Taking off, I ran to the back of the nearest house, hopping over a couple of fences, and making my way to a different block. It was a maneuver I had done dozens of times as a little kid—like when I ran from Ziggy's Wagon—but now the stakes were much higher.

After a minute of running and jumping, I stopped to catch my breath and thought two things: 1) *I'm way too old for this shit* and 2) *I need to get the fuck out of Syracuse.*

* * *

For the next couple weeks, Shayan and I developed an intricate strategy for dealing with Johnny Sabs: We hid. The long Thanksgiving Break helped. But when school was back in session, I knew I had to get away.

"I can't hide in a dorm," was the last thing I said to Shai before skipping town for a week. "I have to be out there. On the street, and on the bus," I continued. "At my parents'." He agreed it was a wise move.

I had invited myself along to see Phish with Craig, whose friend from home Kristin came from SUNY Albany to drive him to a few Phish shows. Craig reluctantly agreed to bring me along under one condition: NO ACID. That was perfectly fine with me. After all, doctor's orders. So, I put off going to the registrar's office while we hit up arenas in Hershey, New Haven, Niagara Falls, and Cleveland before ending up at Albany's Knickerbocker Arena on December 9th.

Each winter, the cities of Upstate New York "compete" over who gets the most amount of total snow. The perverse Golden Snowball Award bestows upon its winner bragging rights for a full year, and as I stood outside the Knick, I thought, I thought Albany should win early by virtue of technical knockout. It was 9 a.m. I had walked here from Kristin's while everyone was still sleeping, and I was ill prepared for the bitter cold. With my Converse sneakers, yellow jacket, t-shirt, and no gloves, I situated myself outside the loading dock waiting for the band to arrive in their tour buses for their inevitable sound check, ready to hand to them my letter. I had tried at each of the shows we went to the past couple weeks, and this was my final shot.

Between the perforated dot matrix pages, I conveyed my conviction that Phish—whether they knew it or not—was in a position to make a difference. I explained how they had already changed my life and pleaded for them to acknowledge the power they had over their fans and to capitalize on it for the better good.

I waited for a very long time, occasionally walking around to keep my toes from freezing but always returning to the loading dock hoping to spot a band member. But eventually, fans started to arrive. Drinks were opened, pipes were loaded, and the scent of grilled cheese filled the air. The letter would once again have to wait. I searched for my friends—Craig, Kristin, Stapes, who took a Greyhound from Syracuse, and Amanda, another one of Craig's high school friends I hadn't met but whose dorm we were crashing at. Stapes and Craig were dreading this because they thought she was super annoying. They warned that she might talk my ear off.

While searching the parking garage, I came across a huge, 1950's era Aerocoach bus that had the words "Peacemaker" across its front. I'd seen it at several shows but had no clue what it was or why it was there. Its inhabitants, who looked more like farmers than hippies, would hand out a black and white newspaper after shows, whose cover was graced by angelic illustrations of Janis Joplin, Jimi Hendrix, and Jerry Garcia. A sign on the back said, "We know the way, we'll bring you home." But it was a handwritten "free hot tea" note on the dashboard that compelled me to trepidatiously step on board.

The bus was cozy and quiet, a stark contrast to the scene outside. Years of hearing my dad talking about his craft gave me enough sense to understand that the wood used to line the walls was expensive. The chairs and booths were quality leather, and the tall ceilings were cathedral-like. Copper lamps provided the type of quiet and atmospheric light one might find in a Vanderbilt-era library. What had I walked into?

Three older men wearing Guatemalan print sweaters and a woman in her twenties sat around, talking. None of them looked particularly happy, but they described to me their way of life with the convictions of those who believed they had truly figured out the world. As Elijah, the youngest of the group, explained to me, they were part of a fifty-year-old community in Vermont called the Twelve Tribes.

Elijah? Twelve Tribes? These words, so closely ingrained in Judaism, resonated deep within me, and I was intrigued. Elijah continued to explain that for years the tribes had been sending some of their "family" on Dead tour in an effort to "help others who desire to bring peace to this dying world." Was this group what I had been looking for? A new way of living, of thinking, and of working towards a better future for all? I was eager to hear more.

The more questions I asked, the more I wanted to know. And half an hour later, I was picturing myself living this simple but rewarding life in Vermont. But when I asked about their families, it became clear that most tribe members cut off contact with them for one reason or another. I thought of my own family, especially my dad, and how hurt they would be if I were to do the same.

While I was lost in thought, Elijah asked if I wanted to stay on the bus with them up in Maine. I could even finish up the tour with them. There was only one week left, and I could go up and visit their farm afterward. It was tempting. I was done with classes, and it would get me away from Johnny Sabs. Perhaps it was even part of some preordained plan.

But after hearing more about their day-to-day life on the farm, terms like "communal property" and things that sounded like they came from the New Testament made me hyper suspicious. I thought of the cults lecture from that USY event. I got out of there—fast.

I'VE FALLEN, AND I CAN'T GET UP

When Syracuse Savings Bank opened in 1876, it was the tallest building in the city and the first with an elevator. Its majestic structure, now a Key Bank, spoke of much grander days, and its enormous lobby made me self-conscious. While my efforts to get Phish my letter failed, I was relieved to focus on two very important things: officially withdrawing from my classes and paying back Johnny Sabs. I was lucky to have avoided him for that long, and I had a Hail Mary idea that involved this bank.

My Bar Mitzvah took place on September 1, 1990, four days after my thirteenth birthday. The extensive preparation leading up to it consisted of fifty percent Torah studying and fifty percent explaining to my friends what the hell a Bar Mitzvah was. I wasn't exactly sure myself, but I knew it was a huge deal because it would be my first time being in the same room with all of my siblings since my sister's wedding when I was three. I also was aware that people would be giving me money. In fact, by the end of the night, I was nearly three thousand dollars richer—a fortune. Five years later and with a couple weeks left in the semester, I took the bus here from Westcott to try to take it out.

My parents had put the funds away in a custodial savings account, set aside for some yet-to-be-determined grand expense. As far I was concerned, the grand expense was here. So with my OCC ID and social security card in hand, I asked to speak with the manager, hoping that because I was now eighteen, the money was mine. But, as the smug, balding man in glasses explained, that wasn't exactly the case.

I pleaded and argued. "But it's *my* account."

"Technically that's true. Sort of. But you need your parents, as they are the custodians."

"But I'm eighteen now." I was repeating myself, which I knew would get me nowhere.

"I understand. But you still need your parents. I'm sorry," he said before turning to a waiting client.

I exited the bank, dejected, and went to the main Centro bus hub a few blocks away. Like the Syracuse Savings Bank building, this part of downtown had marks of magnificent days, with its old movie palace and Art Deco buildings. But everything was falling apart and depressing. The streets that were once packed with people going about their day were now transient, a place for those without a car to transfer buses. Like me, now on my way to Onondaga Hill.

The administration and governance building at OCC was dingy and unorganized. The line was long. I was far from the only one here for some issue, concern, or to plead a case. The secretary, who was busy shuffling papers and looking half asleep when I asked to withdraw from all my classes, didn't even look up when informing me I was late. The deadline to drop classes was November 20th. I didn't even know there was a deadline.

I tried talking her into making an exception. Watching my mom insist that teachers not hold me back all those years taught me it was possible to bend the will of any administration. So, I placed my student ID on the counter and did my best to convince this lady, and when she sensed a growing anger in my tone, she dropped what she was doing, looked me dead in the eye, and informed me in no uncertain terms that was not going to happen. As she went back to her paperwork, my blood boiled. I felt the people in line behind me wondering if I would cause a scene and if it would hold up their day. But I collected myself, accepted my fate of a zero point zero GPA, and started to walk out with my head held as high as possible.

I was almost out when the staff member called after me, "Wait, one minute." A whiff of hope caused every hair on my body to stand up. I turned around, surprising even myself that I had the ability to talk my way through that.

"You forgot your ID," she said with an annoyed look on her face.

* * *

I couldn't get out of bed the next morning, not that I slept much. Samantha, Johnny Sabs, my 0.0 GPA. All of it on my mind. The most pressing thing, though, was Phish. The thoughts swirling around my head since Chicago were now all-consuming.

I wanted clarity. I needed to know if I was going insane. And the only person able to help—other than the band itself—was Petta.

While some aspects of that night were clearly figments of my imagination, others, like communicating telepathically with Petta, could in theory be verified with the man himself. And with the fall tour now over, I abandoned the notion of getting my letter to the band. But I was still convinced there was more to Phish than music and that I had a role in figuring it out. I was hoping that recounting the night with Petta would provide clues to figure out my next step.

At some point before noon, I sat up and checked my beeper. There were several pages from Shayan, two "911's" and a "187," meaning either he wanted to kill me or someone was about to kill us. I quickly got up, and after a change of clothes, went down to the front door. My mom, reading the paper on the dining room table, called after me with another one of her police blotter name guessing games. I simply said, "Not today," as I put my shoes on and left.

Walking up The Mount, gasping from the dry winter air, two SU security sedans drove by me on their way down. I picked up my pace and hoped to God those cars had nothing to do with us. My concern grew to confusion when I saw that Flint now had security who required an SU ID to get in—just like at Brewster Bowland, the hood-adjacent dorm where Lenny lived. I was unable to get inside, but it didn't take long to spot a familiar face. Erin immediately ran over to sign me in, frantically asking if I'd heard what happened. Arriving on the fourth floor, I saw a few people I knew, and they all looked at me like they'd seen a ghost. I hoped Shayan was okay.

I was relieved to find Shai nervously pacing around his room, all in one piece. But without saying anything, he pointed to the direction of Samantha's room, and half a second later, I was out the door, Shai calling after me, "I wouldn't go in there right now." I saw why: Kara was sitting on her bed crying, traumatized. A few of her art school friends were consoling her. Samantha was nowhere to be found.

"You," she said to me with a frightening amount of intensity. "This is because of you!" Her voice was now raised to one tiny notch below screaming. "And you!" she continued, directed at Shai, who tugged at my arm to get the hell out of there.

"Townie!" she screamed through the door, as Shai and I bolted back to his room. He explained that around midnight, Johnny Sabs came looking for him. He somehow knew, presumably from Polish, not only what room Shai lived in, but who we hung out with. And once a scared-out-of-his-mind Tyler informed the fat son of a bitch that Shai was at Harry's with the DU guys, he went straight to Samantha's room. He didn't have to travel very far.

Kara was on her way to the bathroom when Johnny grabbed her, thinking she was Samantha. According to someone who had heard it from someone who was told directly from Kara, he lifted up his shirt to expose the butt of a gun, smiled, and said, "This is a message for Shai and your hippie boyfriend." Shayan and I were in disbelief. Thankfully, the actual police were not notified. The university definitely did not want this getting out to the public.

"We gotta find Lamar," Shai said adamantly. "Before we go on break." I nodded in agreement.

"I'll meet you out front in an hour."

"Where you going?"

"To find out if I'm crazy."

I hadn't been to Petta's since the beginning of the school year, but there were legendary stories of what went down here. Some jokingly warned to wear a condom under your clothes just to step foot in there. But, at this moment, it seemed like any other dorm room. The two of us sat there smoking stogs and drinking 40's of Woodchuck Cider as we went over Halloween moment-by-moment.

Petta remembered our telepathic conversation exactly as I did, but he didn't remember much that happened after the lights went down. He vividly recalled his line about "the bait," and, of course, me getting naked. He also said that as long as he lived, he would never forget finding me shackled to a wall—the craziest thing he'd ever seen.

Recounting that night was mentally taxing, and as I lit up another Marlboro Light, Petta went to use the bathroom. While I was sitting there watching the smoke drift out of my hand, I noticed a message that his roommate had scribbled on a small white board near the telephone. "Samantha called." And there it was.

Before Petta came back, I barged into Shai's room, interrupting a studious and now very annoyed Tyler. The look on Shai's face told me all I needed to know about Petta and Samantha. I prodded Shai on why he didn't tell me. "I didn't have the heart."

A DOSE OF REALITY

* * *

Shayan and I walked to Lamar's dorm eager to get our hands on our money or on him. We needed this to happen before the end of the semester, when everyone would be home from college. At that point, it would be easy for Johnny to find us at any of the many class of '95 house parties or get-togethers. As we walked, the urban landscape shifted dramatically from cozy campus to urban grit. Nearby, towering housing projects and downtown factories emitted dark smoke into the sky, mixing with the clouds, rendering it impossible for any sun to get through. Not that there was much sun to begin with.

"Yo, what were you talking about the other night—when you got back from Chicago?"

I knew I had sounded crazy, and I was mad that I said anything in the first place. But I was excited, and it just came out. I brushed it off as nothing, but Shai knew me better than that.

"I haven't told you the full story about what happened, yet, but …" How was I going to explain this? "Look at how much I've changed because of Phish."

He looked me up and down. "Only difference I see is the new jacket."

He laughed, but I didn't.

"No, I know," he relented.

We reverted to walking in silence.

"Yo, promise you're not going to turn into one of the crazy people on Westcott," he said. There was nothing I could do but laugh with him.

We were a couple blocks from Brewster Bowland when a young black man in a hoodie approached. From the look of his face, he hadn't slept in a day or two, and the hand he kept in his pocket was likely clutching a weapon.

"Yo man, let me get five dollars," he demanded, pulling his arm from his pocket as if to strike. But his demeanor suddenly changed, and he took his hood off and smiled. It was Henry Breland, the kid I had passed the Sears catalog to years ago. I hadn't seen him since he dropped out in eighth grade. He was going through hard times—not all that surprising considering the last I saw him he was selling rock. We chatted for a few minutes and then went on our way.

Brewster and Bowland were connected by an expansive plaza that could have been similar to Mount Olympus, if the surroundings and facilities weren't in such disarray. Another big difference was its twenty-four-seven security—really just a student who checked IDs at the door. We had somehow forgotten about this, but after a few minutes of pleading, Shai convinced the dude manning the security table to let us both through.

Shai knocked hard on Lamar's door. Eventually, his chubby Puerto Rican roommate appeared, obviously unaware of what Lamar was involved with. Otherwise, he wouldn't have told us to check the game room. We quickly thanked him and nearly sprinted down to the basement's recreation facilities.

The concrete hallway leading to the game room was narrow, and the sounds of arcade games and pool balls echoed throughout. The main door was made of thick metal, and a tall but narrow window allowed us to peek through. We scanned the space, trying to avoid being spotted, when we saw Lamar in the far end corner playing ping pong with an Asian kid. Lamar was no match for his competitor, and when the ball flew past him, he stepped out of our view to retrieve it. This was our chance to get in there and grab him.

When Shai and I barged in, we bumped into a loud group of girls. When we got untangled, we saw one very confusing-looking Asian dude standing there while Lamar fled through a back door. We went after him, but it was pointless. He could have been anywhere—on the quad, in some random person's room. Who knew? But there was one thing we were now absolutely sure of: He wasn't giving us our money back. At least not willfully. And not before the end of the semester.

FRIENDS DON'T LET FRIENDS DRIVE DRUNK

The last few days of the semester went out with a whimper. Once finals hit, people left one or two at a time until all at once the dorms were empty. Samantha left without so much as a goodbye. Kara went home the day after the Johnny Sabs incident and was probably not coming back.

It was almost Christmas, and Shai's floor was eerily silent. The hall that was always filled with chatter, excitement, and lively conversation was now overwhelmed by the steady hum of fluorescent lights. The sound of traffic finding its way through fortified windows. The syncopated buzz of a lonely vending machine.

Shayan was the only student who stayed for break, save for a few RAs. He stayed because it was a safe shelter from Johnny Sabs. It also kept Tammy's psycho ass out of his hair. Lastly, it gave The Crew a place to get fucked up.

It was nearly midnight, and me, Jonah, Will, Joe, and Elias were sitting around Shayan's room with forties, blasting Wu-Tang Clan. We were bringing each other up to speed on our respective new friends and all the stories that go along with being a college freshman. The Halloween ordeal was mentioned a couple times, but it was clear people were trying to skirt the subject. I think they were afraid to hear how nuts I would sound.

We'd been getting fucked up like this every night of winter break. We didn't have fake IDs to get into bars, we were bored of Zopie's, and it was way too cold to drink in the woods. Anyway, that didn't matter. It was just nice to have everyone home. And there had been no sign of Johnny Sabs—not here, not on Westcott, not anywhere.

Earlier in the day, I made pot brownies. We were familiar with the urban legend that ganja-infused confectionaries got you super stoned, but we'd never actually seen it done. So when I came across a book at Seven Rays that explained the technique, I tried it out. I was hoping it'd be a nice substitute for acid, which I vowed to never do again. The recipe worked like a charm; we were way beyond stoned.

"Every morning, she makes me get up," Jonah complained about his mom, a high school teacher at Nottingham. His eyes were completely bloodshot. "It's like, I'm on break, let me sleep in."

"That's insane. How early?" asked Elias.

"I don't know. Noon maybe—"

Suddenly there was a hard knock on the door. We ditched our forties in various nooks and sprayed air freshener. It was Shai's RA, and she was pissed.

"Music's pretty loud," she said, scanning the room suspiciously. She was referring to the Wu-Tang CD we were blasting.

"Sorry, I'll turn it down." As Shai got up, the room fell silent—well, except for Method Man yelling "*I'll fuckin' sew your asshole closed, and keep feedin' you, and feedin' you, and fee—*" He shut it off.

"Everything okay?" the RA prodded.

"Yeah, yeah. For sure," Shai answered nervously, motioning to a plate of half-eaten brownies on his nightstand. "We're eating brownies."

There was a long pause while we figured out if she was buying it or not.

"I love brownies," she asked as she walked towards the nightstand. "Can I have one?"

We all looked at each other, like, *What now?*

"Are you guys students? I don't recognize yo—"

Clink. Her foot knocked over a forty bottle, spilling its contents everywhere.

"My shoes!" she screeched, taking a pad and pen from her back pocket to write Shai up.

* * *

We had nowhere to go after leaving the dorms. Packed like sardines in Joe's busted old Volvo, we parked at the only place that would never let anyone down—any time of the day, through rain, sleet, hail, and snow: Wegmans. We spent a couple hours passing aisles of fresh produce and pontificating how the world would be better if everyone conducted their lives like the company, whose focus on quality, service, and work culture was legendary. I wasn't sure if the brownies were making me paranoid, but I was sure Shai and the guys were talking about me. Talking about what happened in Chicago. Perhaps even worried I was losing my mind.

"I want you guys to hear something," I said. "Let's go back to the car."

Once I brought up Halloween, it was obvious everyone wanted to talk about it but didn't know how. They had all heard, either briefly from me over the phone or from someone else in The Crew, that I once again had a bad trip that landed me in the hospital. Word was I believed Phish was part of some conspiracy, and that I possibly had delusions of grandeur. They weren't that far off.

I tried to explain what happened in Chicago, but the way they stared reminded me of the Nottingham cafeteria when I didn't know about the SATs and sang the praises of community college. Ironically, I was explaining that for the first time in my life, I wanted to excel in school.

But enough with the talk. I pulled out a Maxwell tape that I'd been waiting weeks for and handed it to Joe. The handwritten label read, "Phish: Rosemont Horizon 10/31/95."

The quality of the tape was crappy, but when the crowd cheered at the start of the show, I was transported back to Chicago. It was my first time listening to a recording of the night, and it was validating to hear *"Icculus," "Divided Sky," "Wilson,"* and *"Free."* We listened as enormous plows ushered snow into impossibly large piles in the nearly deserted, football-field-sized parking lot. As I relayed what was going through my mind that night, even they had to admit it was understandable how someone in my shoes could interpret shit that way. Was I really so crazy?

When the sun came up hours later, we drove to Nottingham to watch the younger kids showing up to school. We got there a good forty-five minutes before the first bell, and the parking lot was empty. But it didn't take long to fill up. And when a familiar blue Dodge minivan parked right next to us, our mouths dropped. It was Jonah's mom. And since Jonah was sitting shotgun, he was the first thing she saw after taking her keys out of the ignition.

None of us knew how we should, or how she would, react. Looking at her son crammed in with the rest of us blurry-eyed fools, she simply shook her head in disappointment. Jonah made eye contact with her and, without blinking, rolled down his window, and said, "I'm up early."

* * *

"Spring semester" was a tauntingly cruel name for the school session that began in the most brutal part of winter and ended in the first week of April, when it was not unusual for Syracuse to still have snow on the ground. As I walked past Harry's bar in early 1996, the line outside was even longer and more obnoxious than usual. It was a typical January night, somewhere around thirty degrees, yet the parade of identically dressed girls would suggest otherwise. Their skirts barely covered their asses, and their tops weren't any more substantive.

As the girls shivered in place, desperate to get in, I stared at their jet-black, straight hair. Not sure how I'd missed it before, but damn they looked good. Old Dirty Bastard's "Shimmy Shimmy Ya'll" blared through the main door, and I wondered if Shai was in there; he loved that song. As I cut across the line, a couple of gelled-up dudes looked pissed—they thought I was trying to cut them. But while it was a Saturday night, there would be no partying for me. I was going to Zopie's to study.

I was on academic probation and lost my right to matriculate as a music major—or any major—until I pulled myself up academically. That wasn't really a concern, though, because my goal was to get good enough grades to transfer to film school at either USC or UCLA.

The atmosphere inside Zopie's was stark and moody, and except for an REM CD playing, it was quiet as a library. I looked around at the hipper-than-thou crowd reading or quietly chatting, and I thought a year ago I would have looked at them as weirdos or, at best, nerds. Now I wanted to be one of them. I sat down and opened my textbook on *The Films of Alfred Hitchcock.*

I had no idea how I was going to suddenly, for the first time in my life, do well in school. But taking interesting classes sounded like a good start. The Hitchcock class was taught by Doug Brode, a film critic for the local NBC affiliate. He had a way of weaving the real world into his lectures, using films to touch upon history, philosophy, science, psychology, and more into the movies we watched.

I rummaged through my backpack, took out a yellow marker, and highlighted the first sentence that sounded important, making a squeaking noise that annoyed a girl next to me. She was reading something called Kafka. I continued to read and highlight, the first page now a sea of bright yellow. I had no idea what I was doing. The Kafka chick stared at me like I was an idiot and was moving to another table when a familiar face sat down next to me. It was Robbie Cornbloom with a big grin on his face.

Robbie moved to California after graduation, and I hadn't seen him in nearly a year. He was back in town for a couple of weeks and was totally amused to see me studying, recalling when I ripped up my report card in second grade and said I would go to OCC and worry about grades then. Well, here we were ten years later. Robbie sensed something in me had changed, and I wanted to tell him what had happened in the past few months. I wanted him to know I was going to change the world, even if I was unsure exactly how. But instead I just told him I had big plans, and that one day he'd find out what they were.

After Robbie left, I got into a studying groove, and the next thing I knew, it was nearly eleven and Zopie's was getting ready to close. When a loud crash came from the other side of the room, I assumed it was some pots and pans as the kitchen staff wound down. But then a commotion formed outside, from Harry's, and it was a sound I knew all too well from my days in the Nottingham cafeteria. A fight—and a big one. And just like at 'Ham, I got up to take a look. A bunch of Harry's people were running away, with Shayan right along with them. He was pledging his fraternity at Harry's when Johnny Sabs came looking for him. When word quickly spread that he had a gun, it nearly caused a stampede.

As a result of that night, Shai was "blackballed" from the frat. There would be no Drugs Unlimited for him.

* * *

By February, Syracuse had settled into a coating of white and gray. As I stood alone in the far south end of a snow-covered BB plaza, the hood over my head not only kept my ears from falling off but also provided anonymity. That's when I saw what I was waiting for: Lamar walking across the plaza in a new puffy North Face jacket. I wanted to wring my hands around his fucking neck. There was a lot of space for him to run, so I waited to act. But once he was close enough to the doors that there would be nowhere to go, I walked towards him—slowly at first and then quickly. As I picked up the pace, the packed snow squeaked under my feet, alerting Lamar to my presence. He took off towards the entrance, past the security table.

Lamar walked in displaying his ID card, confident he had gotten away, but I was quick to flash my own—Stapes let me borrow his. The motherfucker made a beeline for an emergency exit and was—poof—gone. But that was fine, because I knew exactly where he was. I took my sweet time making my way through that emergency door, knowing that Shai had been waiting for him.

The industrial hallway had exposed piping along the ceiling. Lamar was so tall that when Shai had him jacked up against the wall, his head was almost touching the pipes. At this moment, weeks of frustration and anger coalesced into a fit of rage, and I went up and punched him in the mouth, to both his and Shai's surprise.

Lamar was ranting about how his customers weren't paying up and that someone had stolen an ounce from his room. He sounded sincere, but anyone in his shoes would have said the same thing. He looked at Shai, and then to me, and then back to Shai for some sort of compassion or sympathy. But when he saw he wouldn't be getting any from either of us, he told us that while he couldn't pay us, there was something else he could provide. Something other than money that might protect us from Johnny Sabs, who he knew all about.

"What?" Shai asked.

It's in my room."

"Oh, hell no," I offered. "You think we're stupid?"

"I'm serious. Look, take my keys. They're in my pocket."

I grabbed the keys out of Lamar's pocket as Shai continued to hold him. At that moment, a sheepish student walked by, trying to figure out what to make of the situation. He looked like he might go and ask for help, so I came up with a cover. "Naw, man," I said to Lamar with a fake smile. "You gotta say it with more emotion!" Then I turn to the student. "Drama club."

Lamar's room was bare. The only decoration on his side was a Notorious BIG poster that was haphazardly taped to a wall. A small TV and Super Nintendo sat beside cheap cologne and some deodorant. As soon as we walked in, Lamar went over to his desk and opened a drawer.

"Check it out."

Shai and I looked inside the desk, where we saw a notebook, calculator, a couple of pens, and, finally, one small pistol. "This is all I can give you," he said. "For now."

BE ALL THAT YOU CAN BE

The cemetery where Shai and I first met with Johnny Sabs had frozen over, making it even more creepy. It was now early February, and the past ten weeks felt more like ten years. As we sat, steam escaped our mouths with every breath. We arranged to meet Johnny here, but we didn't really have a plan for when he showed up—just to come clean and beg to make it up to him. The effort was certainly doomed to fail. The more likely scenario was that he would not come alone, he would not hear us out, and he would not hesitate to fuck us up. That's why we had the gun.

Tired and weary, I sat against a tree trunk. Shai went to do the same but had to make some adjustments after remembering the piece in his waistband. There we sat quietly for a long time, until it began to snow.

"How about that," Shai said. "It's snowing in Syracuse."

I laughed.

"How's classes going?"

"Good question. I'm trying, that's for sure."

"Well, that's already an exponential improvement."

It was true.

"You know what exponential means, right?" he joked, as we both cracked up.

I hinted to Shai why I was so motivated to do well in school. I didn't give any specifics but told him there were grand plans in store.

"Let me guess," he inquired. "It involves Phish." A beat before I answered yes.

"Dude, what is up to you?" Shai was irritated. "You're losing your shit, you know that?"

I was incensed at his anger, but both of us shut the hell up when headlights illuminated the landscape. As we stood, Shai looked down to ensure the gun wasn't showing. I swallowed hard as the car approached. We expected Johnny's Cougar, but it was a maintenance vehicle that proceeded to drive right past us. As the snow came down harder, I pulled my jacket tighter around me, the cold taking its toll.

"Bet you wish you had your Starter jacket."

We laughed in a way we hadn't in a long time. And we needed it. But by 9:30, the snow was sticking, and we wanted to get the hell out of there. By 10:00, it was clear this was a serious snowstorm and that Johnny Sabs was not going to show. With an immense sense of relief, we headed back up The Mount to Shai's room.

* * *

Nearly a month went by without a word from Johnny Sabs. We still had no clue why he didn't show up that night, but one thing was for certain: He could chase us all he wanted, but we weren't gonna chase him.

With Johnny at least temporarily out of the picture, I was able to focus on school, where I seemed to be doing well. I mean, it was March—nearly six weeks into the semester—and I hadn't missed a single class. But when Stapes and Craig told me they were going to Binghamton for an acoustic Dave Matthews show, a brand-new format for the suddenly popular singer, I took the weekend off from studying and joined them.

One year prior, I stumbled upon a Dave Matthews Band show at Syracuse's Landmark Theater, an old 1930s movie palace. At that time, DMB had just opened for the Dead, and the audience full of dreadlocked hippies reflected that. There was none of the white-hat wearing, booze-guzzling, PDA-loving crowd that it would become known for.

But since that night at the Landmark, DMB's popularity skyrocketed, their shows a scene of drunken mayhem. So it was exciting when Dave announced a low-key night with only him and his unknown friend Tim Reynolds in a small college auditorium. I took a bus there with Stapes and Craig, planning to spend the night at Amanda's place, a proposition the two of them were once again dreading. While they were not at all happy to see her, they were more than excited for the mushrooms she had. When Craig wasn't looking, I was offered a half gram, and since it wasn't a Phish show and it wasn't acid, I knew it would be okay to eat at that modest amount.

The basement-like gym that doubled as an auditorium was a standing room only yet intimate affair. Unlike the show I had seen a year ago, there was no dancing. The audience was attentive. About a third of the way into the one-set concert, Dave and Tim played the dark and mysterious song "Minarets," whose middle eastern tinged chords were peppered with intense lyrics touching upon religion, war, and human nature. That song shifted my pleasant and complacent trip into something more substantial. The mushrooms were taking my mind along for a ride.

As the song's jam section grew louder and more abstract, I asked myself what had I accomplished since Halloween? What was it all for? I had not been able to deliver that letter to the band, so now what? I was attempting to do well in school, and yet, here I was once again, tripping out at a concert instead of doing homework or otherwise being responsible. It was typical E.R.—fucking up as always.

Thankfully, the song ended and the wild applause snapped me out of it. I sat the next tune out and went for a walk around the lobby, assuring myself it was only the shrooms talking and that I had everything under control. I took a deep breath and walked back to the auditorium entrance. But when I opened the door, the sounds and lights of everything going on inside wrapped around me in a serpentine-like motion, forcing me back into the concert against my will. My field of vision froze, and I felt that same door from Rosemont Horizon begin to open. And once again the lights came together to form a graphic—"We interrupt your regularly scheduled programming to bring you this special." There was no point in resisting.

While months had passed since Rosemont Horizon, I was right back in the same place. I sensed everyone staring at me, applauding just like they did on *This is Your Life*. Holy shit, it *was* real. It was *not* all in my head. Instead of being relieved that I wasn't hallucinating after all, I was overcome with shame and panic. How did I let this happen once again? Hypnotized by Guyute and scared of what would happen next, I was summoned up, along with others who were attuned this evening, to receive the next chapter in our collective journey. This time to the song "Typical Situation."

It's a typical situation,
in these typical times,
too many choices …

Those words served as a reminder of the dire times we live in. How my peers were all consumed with materialism and blinded to the realities of the world. I now knew that the purpose of what happened in Chicago was not about me. It was not about Phish. It was about *us*. Yes, I was undergoing an incredible transformation, and Phish certainly played their role in that, but we were here together as part of an alliance. For those still unattuned, it was all a typical situation, and it was on us to help them awaken.

Everybody's happy,
everybody's free,
WE'LL KEEP THE BIG DOOR OPEN,
everyone'll come around …

As the song picked up to an uplifting and inspiring pace, the docile crowd stood up in a choreographed-like way and danced. It was too much for me; I didn't want to be part of any movement. I didn't want to fall into a trance. So, I went back into the lobby only to see the security team putting up barriers and locking the exits. Their matching shirts, flashlights, and walkie talkies made the scene seem conspiratorial, like they were going to prevent us, the attuned, from leaving. But just when I thought there was no way out, I saw an emergency exit propped open and knew it was my chance to escape. If security caught me, I thought, who knew what would happen? Perhaps I'd end up in the hospital again, with a needle in my arm to make me believe this was all in my imagination.

Once again, I found myself on the outskirts of a concert venue on a freezing night without a jacket, tripping hard. But as I walked farther from the venue onto a snow-white grassy knoll leading into the parking lot, thoughts connected in my mind, forming the larger picture of what this was really about. This wasn't only a movement; this was war—the likes of which the world hadn't seen in decades.

This was no conventional war, not like the ones we read about in school or that my dad had experienced. It was a subconscious conflict that most people didn't even know was happening. Instead of guns, bombs, and armies, it was music, movies, and media conglomerates. At stake were the minds and souls of humanity. I stood there, taking in the severity of the situation, when Stapes approached me, my yellow jacket in hand.

Stapes tried to calm me down, but I was focused on the new global conflict. The enemy was unknown. It had likely been with us since the dawn of time—some called it evil. And the first and most crucial battle was to get people to see that this was even happening in the first place. Not only was the public oblivious to their hypnosis, they reveled in it. The force that stood to destroy civilization was used by popular culture to put humanity in a trance, consumed by consumerism and the primal desires that humanity had spent centuries trying to erase.

The ambiguity about what went down in Chicago was now clear. I was to play a major role in all of this. I would become CEO of a major media conglomerate and do to the masses what Phish did to me—program and then deprogram them publicly to illustrate to the world how corporations and their mass media brainwashed them into unwittingly joining a cult—the cult of materialism. This would ensure it would never happen again. I turned to Stapes, relieved that I now knew the truth.

"So, this is World War III we're talking about," I said, convinced we were on the same page. A moment passed while Stapes tried to make sense of that. "Is my dad one of the good guys or the bad guys?" I asked.

Even this far outside the gym, you could hear the crowd erupt as Dave spoke to the audience before the encore. While it was impossible to understand what he was saying, the tone in his voice was reminiscent of Trey and the "Icculus" narration. It was the same voice from Rosemont Horizon—the angry vocals of Rage Against the Machine frontman Zach De La Rocha. Then it hit me: This was all one movement.

Phish was how I found my role in the fight, but there were other scenes involved. Dave Matthews was one of them, bringing in the "White Hat" crowd. There was also Rusted Root, and probably several other artists whose missions—whether intentional or unwittingly—were getting the message across and recruiting those to the cause. Rage was the most obvious—there was no obfuscation in their songs. That's why I saw Trey turn into Zach De La Rocha in Chicago, and that's why I was hearing him on stage with Dave Matthews now.

"Rage Against the Machine is on stage?" I asked Stapes.

"Come on, buddy. Let's go," he replied, worried I was about to take my clothes off and start clicking my heels together. We were going to the parking lot when Craig and Amanda approached. They had been looking for us.

"Hey, you doing okay?" Amanda asked. I was so out of it that I didn't even know who she was. My friends were concerned. I looked at Amanda again, trying to place her. And when she looked into my eyes and smiled, a lightbulb finally went off. I could see Stapes and Craig visibly relieved that I recognized her.

"Oh, right," I said. "You're Amanda, the girl Craig and Stapes always talk shit about."

Once we got back to the Binghamton dorms, Stapes, Craig, and Amanda went to an after party, while I stayed alone to let the trip wind down. I analyzed the night, the Rosemont Horizon show, and the months between. When Trey sang "I see the path ahead of me," I thought I knew what that path was. But it was only now that I fully grasped it. I would not tell anyone about the war or my role in it—not a single soul—for fear that the wrong people would find out and try to stop me.

My next steps? To find the other attuned and then go from there.

***

A few days after the Dave Matthews concert, Cholo woke me up with huge licks to the face, which I happily accepted but motioned that I wanted to go back to sleep. I had just begun to doze off again when CeCe called up from the bottom of the stairs.

"Do you know Juan Sabatino Acosta?" she asked, struggling to pronounce the name correctly. The sound of the police blotter crinkling in her hand set me off. I stood up and yelled across the room and down the stairs.

"Stop asking me about this shit!" I was furious and couldn't remember the last time I'd yelled at her like that.

"Okay, honey. I was just asking," she mumbled while walking back down to the first floor. And then it hit me.

"Wait," I said to myself, running down the stairs as Cholo nipped at my feet.

The paper sat on the kitchen table. I picked it up to make sure it said what I thought it did. Juan Sabatino Acosta was arrested for possession of half a pound of cocaine, four pounds of marijuana, and for the possession of four firearms, including a semi-automatic rifle. Stunned, I put down the paper and thought about what that all meant. I hadn't heard the name Juan Acostas in a couple years, but I definitely remembered his nickname.

It was Johnny Sabs.

"Nice!" I said to myself with a fist pump before picking up the phone to tell Shai the news. But when Shai picked up the phone I could tell something was wrong.

"Come by my mom's house," was all he said.

The thick stack of papers sat like a dossier on the desk in Shai's childhood bedroom. In fact, that's exactly what it was—a case against Shayan. There were dozens of citations by resident advisors, on everything from smoking pot in his room to urinating in a stairwell. I knew he once woke up in the middle of the night to pee in Samantha's bong, but I didn't know about the stairwell. The phrase "local friends" was mentioned dozens of times. At least they didn't say townie. They also mentioned that he shattered an empty forty bottle in the hallway after a 'Cuse men's basketball loss.

The report didn't stop there. There were also numerous complaints filed by other students about his local friends coming in and out. There were mentions of drug dealing. Even Shai's own roommate had reported him. As I browsed the documents, Shai handed me the ultimate result of all of this: a letter stating he was kicked out—not just from the dorms but from the entire university. The final nail in the coffin was a letter from Kara, who wrote that living near Shayan made her afraid for her life.

Shai was never one to express his emotions, and this was probably the first time I saw him so visibly upset. His parents came to Syracuse to give their son a life closer to what it would have been if not for the Islamic revolution. And Shai had let them, especially his father, down. In the summer, he would enroll at OCC.

Shai wasn't alone. Many of those on The Mount would not return after that first year. There were Reynolds and Kara, who, indeed, never came back. Even Jean Jacket Jenny was gone after being hospitalized for anorexia. Add to that several others who we didn't see again, and my music history teacher's maxim of looking to the left and right applied here too. And although Samantha remained on campus, we had completely lost touch. Someone said she was dating a senior from New Hampshire who liked to do blow on rainy days and drive around in his BMW to see how many pedestrians he could splash on their way home from a night class.

* * *

I spent the next couple months focused on school, and in late May, my transcript arrived. The OCC-branded envelope sat on my dining table, taunting me. Despite my efforts over the past ten weeks, including many turned-in-on-time assignments and solid midterm performances, I didn't know how to feel anything but dread when opening such mail.

I began to rip open the envelope, but decided the occasion called for a butter knife. As I went into the kitchen, Cholo snatched the letter off the table, took it into the TV room, and tore it apart. After chasing him around and snagging it from him, I unfolded it and was astounded. My eighteen-year long streak of C's, D's, and F's had been broken with a near 4.0 GPA. For once, I would be laughing in June.

I spent the first half of the summer taking classes while also soliciting donations door to door for NYPIRG, a local environmental and consumer advocacy group. I saved up a couple hundred bucks and got a ride to Colorado with a friend named Jackie who was moving to California.

The foundation of the Phish scene was the group of young people who followed the band from show to show, and there was a level of mystique in that endeavor. I was sure that underneath the drugs and body odor was a meaningful movement of people who wanted to create change—the attuned from Chicago and Binghamton. I was confident that by going on the 1996 summer tour, I'd meet like-minded individuals who could help me make sense of it all.

After that transcript, my parents couldn't protest this monthlong trip from Colorado to the northernmost tip of New York State. Shai, on the other hand, tried to give me shit for going on tour, but by now he knew it was a lost cause. Perhaps he was relieved I hadn't deteriorated into a full-blown schizophrenic. The last thing he said to me before I left was, "Keep your pants on."

"Don't worry, I'm done with that shit." I promised myself there would be no hallucinogens this summer.

Jackie thought it was weird when I told her she could drop me off on the side of the road near Morrison. But as soon as we pulled off the highway, I saw Craig and Vinnie "Wham" Warner, who took me to their tent in a small vacant field that became a makeshift campground. She saw that this was a real community and that I was in good hands, so off to the West Coast she went.

The Phish scene had grown exponentially in the past two years, and now that Jerry Garcia had passed, many of the Grateful Dead scene's stragglers—its addicts, drug dealers, and homeless kids—simply migrated over to Phish. This unexpectedly large crowd overwhelmed the small town of Morrison. The streets were like a circus twenty-four hours a day, especially at night when the band was performing for the lucky few who actually had tickets. The legendary but very small Red Rocks Amphitheatre was a solid couple miles away in the mountains.

The sweltering days hadn't stopped me from spending all afternoon on the highway ramp, desperately trying to score a ticket from anyone arriving in town. But there were far too many ticketless fans and not an extra in sight. Just when I couldn't take another minute in the sun, a car pulled over and sold me a ticket for fifty bucks. This put a significant dent in my wallet, as I only had about one hundred and thirty five dollars left for the nearly month-long adventure.

The amount of joy and personal satisfaction that came from working my ass off for that ticket was exhilarating, and after smoking a bowl with Craig and Warner in their car, we left our things and went for a stroll in the lot. But after about ten minutes, I became separated from them with my ticket locked in the car, and they were nowhere to be found. About an hour before show time, I was desperate, asking random people if they knew how to pick locks. I considered breaking his window. Eventually, however, I gave up and made my way back to town.

For the next three days, Morrison was overrun with fans and related belligerents. It was a situation the town was ill-prepared for, and by now dozens of cops were on hand to keep the order. I had given up on trying to get into the shows, or even making the hour-long trek to the parking lot. But on the final afternoon, I stumbled upon an old school bus that had been painted head-to-toe in psychedelic patterns like the Further bus of Merry Prankster fame. Sitting on top were familiar faces. It was Sean, Mitch, and Corey, the hippie crew from The Mount. We smoked some weed, which motivated me to try one more time to get into the show.

There was a path at the base of the mountain into which the amphitheater was carved, and while it was massively long and impossible to see where it ultimately led, it appeared to go above and behind the venue and provide a view over the crowd and to the stage. I wasn't the only one up for the challenge of climbing it, as dozens of others had the same idea. These were some of the most real-looking heads I'd ever been around, and their ragged clothing, dreadlocked hair, and gnarly dogs made me optimistic. Were these the others I was supposed to meet? Were these some of the attuned?

Vertigo and altitude sickness kicked in as our small caravan made progress up the mountain. The path became dangerous as we hopped from one rust-colored rock to the next. One bad slip, and it was a hundred feet down. I glanced at a guy who was having trouble making such a jump because his dog was scared shitless. The poor mutt inched towards the edge until the owner picked him up in one big scoop and tossed him to the other side.

The owner held a stack of bumper stickers he had for sale. They read "Heroin Kills, Love Heals." I would soon discover many of these people, and hundreds more like them below in town, were homeless leftovers from Dead tour who didn't care about Phish or the scene. They were known as "gutter punks," here for the drugs and to evade open warrants.

We made it to the mountain top, and when Phish came on, it became an intimate listening party. You could hear the band play, and the roughly forty of us were burning sage, dancing, and having a great time. A vial of liquid acid was passed around, which eventually made its way to me. Man, I wanted to drop some so badly. But I remembered my promise. Besides, if I could do that much damage inside an arena in Chicago, who knew what would happen to me all the way up here? I politely declined.

Dancing to the music, a sense of validation came over me. I made the right choice going on tour. But as I moved by body to the sounds of David Bowie's "Life on Mars"—earlier that day it was reported that NASA discovered strong evidence of microscopic life on the red planet—I saw a young mother injecting herself with a needle while her friend held a baby. All that joy was sucked out of me.

While we were watching the show from high elevation, shit was going down in the town below. Tensions had been brewing between those without tickets and the police for days, and when a cop inadvertently bumped some gutter punk's dog with his patrol car, shit hit the fan. A bottle was thrown at an officer, and dozens of cops showed up in riot gear. By the end of the show, Morrison was totally closed off, leaving hundreds, if not thousands, without a place to go. And those just getting back from the concert, or coming down the mountain like myself, had no way of finding their friends or gathering their things.

At 1:00 a.m., the streets were quiet, and people were let back into town. However, by this point, my friends were nowhere to be found. Craig had a car phone for emergencies, but I didn't know its number. I used my phone card to call his parents from a pay phone, but no one was picking up at that time of night. The temperature had dropped, and no one was around except the occasional police officer on patrol. There was nothing left to do but try to get some sleep on the hard concrete of Morrison's only gas station and figure it all out in the morning.

* * *

It was too cold to sleep in my shorts and Dolphins polo shirt. I shivered on the concrete with my eyes closed, but I just couldn't get them to stay that way. I laid there for hours until at some point in the middle of the night, I must have fallen asleep, because I opened my eyes to find a wisp of sunshine suddenly greeting me. It provided enough heat for a respite and a promise to do right by me as the morning progressed.

Standing up, I discovered an abandoned blanket on the other side of the lot. I wrapped it around myself, cherishing the warmth it provided, and offered to share it with some shivering guy who was in the same situation. As we sat there, waiting for the temperature to rise, I thought of the next show. Phish would be playing at Alpine Valley in Wisconsin—over a thousand miles away—in three days, and I had no way to get there.

Walking through town, it was easy to see that last night's chaos had left many people stranded. There was an older guy, Reggie, who was leading an effort to get a bunch of us stragglers to Alpine Valley. Reggie was short and chubby and sported a fullgrown beard and round Jerry Garcia-esque glasses. At thirtysomething, he became our village elder—and the only one of us old enough to rent a car. More specifically, a Ryder truck.

Sitting in back of a 15 X 8 windowless cage could be stifling. Being there with twenty-five homeless teenagers and four flearidden dogs was a nightmare. I hadn't bathed in several days; for the others, it may have been months. As I sat on the musty floor, I tried not to breathe through my nose. The only source of air came through the partition up front, where Reggie sat shotgun with the window down. I thought of my dad, who had traveled thousands of miles packed in a train with many other families— all without food or water, and with only a hole in the floor to go to the bathroom. From that perspective, the drive from Colorado to Wisconsin should have been a cakewalk.

I glanced around to see a couple directly across from me getting drunk off mouthwash. I refused to believe this was what tour was all about. Perhaps I was being too judgmental. So, I tried to strike up a conversation with a kid next to me, asking if he got into any of the shows.

"I fucking hate Phish," was all he had to say on the matter.

On the way out of Colorado, we stopped off in Boulder for a few hours, as did hundreds of others following the band. The hippie-strong college town was a great place to score pot or shower at the house of an acquaintance. But there would be none of that for me. I considered being dirty as part of the experience. So while others cleaned up and bought provisions for the very long drive in front of us, I walked around town to stretch my legs before the journey *really* began. That's when Mitch, Sean, and Corey's school bus appeared like a mirage. They were all too happy to offer me a ride for the rest of the tour, and so I joined them, along with some other passengers they had picked up along the way, on the spacious, cosmic-feeling ship for the rest of the journey.

Once I was on that bus, my summer experience became more of what I had hoped. Our merry band of misfits also included a sixteen-year-old runaway from Saginaw and a few misfits that didn't fit the hippie mold. We read Kerouac, listened to Johnny Cash, and cooked our own meals using a propane stove on the sides of highways. I got miracled—a free ticket—to many of the shows. Any doubts about being here had vanished, and I was all too happy to be on the road.

IF YOU DON'T KNOW WHO'S KNOCKING, DON'T LET THEM IN

While there were no grand revelations on tour, I came home imbued with a sense of belonging. I also was filthy. But even as I showered for the first time in nearly a month, I kept my head protected underneath a shower cap. After drying off, I stood in front of the mirror with a jar of beeswax and slopped the goop around my hair. I took the knots that had formed naturally and made them even more gnarly. In a week or two, I would have dreadlocks. And they, along with my hemp necklace and patched corduroys, would make me recognizable to any other attuned kids I may encounter—a cultural marker like the Payot of Orthodox Jews.

Three months and a full beard later, I was virtually indistinguishable from, as Shayan liked to say, a homeless person. But despite this appearance, I was on a path towards academic success. My December 1996 transcript was stellar, and I was thinking about applying to film schools for the fall. While originally my plan was to move to LA, I was now so ingrained in the SU culture that it was hard to imagine going anywhere else. So my plan was to stay in Syracuse and attend its film program.

Back at OCC, Professor Brode's lectures were so illuminating that I abandoned my eighteen-year tradition of sitting as far back in the classroom as possible and situated myself in the front row. Today's topic was cultural assimilation as represented in 1950s film. As the son of an immigrant and a mom who grew up in housing projects circa the 1940s, I found the material interesting. Engrossed in the lecture, I glanced up to check the clock and saw the silhouette of a very large man looming in the hallway. And it wasn't Alfred Hitchcock. It was Johnny Sabs. How'd he get out of jail this quickly? I left my books on my desk and got out of the room.

Thankfully, the hallway was empty when I stepped out of class, and I quickly made a beeline for the bathroom. I took a moment to splash water on my face then decided it was best to go back to class and pretend nothing had happened. I'd be safer in there than out here. But as soon as I stepped out of the bathroom, I ran smack into Johnny.

Terrified, I froze. But when this big ass dude said, "Excuse me," in a high-pitched voice, I realized it was all in my mind. Whoever this guy was, he was a dead ringer for the notorious drug dealer, and he had unwittingly scared the shit out of me.

By the time I got back to class, it was over, and I was harkened back to my high school days of roaming the halls to skip school. Brode was the only person left in the classroom, and I was sure he was not happy I'd disappeared like that.

"I want to talk to you." It had been a while since a teacher had said that to me, and it was never good.

"What do you want to do when you're done with this place?" he asked.

I mentioned my plan to transfer to SU's film school. I expected him to be excited, but he cut me off.

"Terrible idea."

Brode explained that SU's film program wasn't a good fit for me. But as he spoke, it made sense. As Brode put it, the film school saw itself as part of the avant-garde, not the Hollywood studio system. If I was intent on staying in Syracuse, he suggested Newhouse's Television, Radio, and Film program. I was a gifted student, he explained, and that track would better suit me.

It was a preposterous idea. Newhouse was an elite institution that admitted some of the country's top students, and unlike USC, UCLA, or even SU, placed full emphasis on academics. There was no creative portfolio as part of the admissions process. How could someone like me get in? The Newhouse reputation in Syracuse was so prolific that even clueless screwups like me knew it was considered the best communications program in the country—and that it was impossible to get into.

Brode explained that he was an adjunct professor at Newhouse and that the school allowed students from other majors at SU to transfer in, provided they had a 3.3 GPA after two semesters and passed a written exam. He offered to write me a letter of recommendation to get my foot in the door at the university, confident his word would get me into their college of arts and sciences. Then it was up to me to bust my ass and get into Newhouse. He urged me to not let him down.

* * *

By winter break, I had two great semesters under my belt and planned to apply to SU's psychology program in the spring. I was confident in my direction, so when Elias offered to drive a bunch of us to DC, Philly, and Boston for Phish's annual four-night holiday run, I didn't think twice. I even brought some ecstasy. The drug, long associated with raves, was overtaking both the campus and Phish scene, as electronic dance music became a counterculture sensation. Rolling on E was great for me because there was little risk of losing my mind. I was able to get my hands on two pills—enough for the first show.

Before the shows, we drove to Long Island to gather with a dozen friends at Craig's house for a night of partying. His parents were out of town, and they never would have known about the shindig if his neighbor hadn't taken one look at me, called Craig's parents, and said there was a guy who "looks like Charles Manson" staying there.

We arrived at the hotel in Philly, a Holiday Inn across the street from The Spectrum. We had booked two rooms for the nine of us, but there was a surprise that I couldn't wait to share. I had called days ago to personally ask for room 420, the newly determined numerical representation of pot. But when we arrived at the hotel, which was packed with concert goers, I was irate to find my request had not been honored. I was beyond disappointed but didn't have too much time to dwell on it, as we wanted to get to the parking lot early.

"What are you taking tonight?" Jonah asked as we gathered our things to head out. I told him about the ecstasy I had brought along.

"If you want to save it for New Year's, I have some chocolate mushrooms."

Oomph. I did not want to be in this position. On one hand, I definitely did not need to be tripping out at a concert, especially not a Phish show. But it would be much more fun to roll on New Year's than on December 29th. And besides, I hadn't taken any psychedelics in ten months. I was doing great in school. And after spending an entire summer tour abstaining, I deserved a reward, no? I dropped the ecstasy in a nightstand drawer and took the shrooms.

There were some spacey moments during the show that were made all the more challenging by the mushroom haze, but I made it through unscathed. Back to the Holiday Inn, however, I became enraged that management had given room 420 to someone else. I called the lobby from our room and demanded to be compensated for this debacle. The manager, who was clearly at her wit's end due to the lobby full of tweakers, was rude to me. It sent me overboard.

"I'll come down there and smack you, ho!" I screamed into the phone before slamming it down and going to sit in Elias' mom's minivan to cool off. Smoking a cigarette in the car, I thought about all that had happened to me since Halloween of the previous year. I had made a breakthrough, for sure, but I still had a long way to go. Yes, I had two amazing semesters, but it was only two, and it was at community college. What if I didn't get into SU? What if I did but couldn't cut it there? Then I got a glimpse of myself in the rearview mirror—the pseudo dreads, the scraggly beard. What was I doing?

I took a long drag off my cigarette and felt the veil of psychosis that had formed in Chicago lifted. Sure, Phish had a lot of eccentric followers who liked to get all fucked up and follow them around, but that was it. There was no conspiracy. There was no mission. There was no fucking World War III.

It was nearly as important of a revelation as Chicago or Binghamton. My delusions were necessary for me to change as a person, but they *were* delusions. And now that I was shedding them, I was on the right path to becoming a responsible, successful, and *sane* adult. But if my goal was still to excel at SU and in the corporate media, I needed to look the part. I needed to blend in. I needed to, thinking back to Brode's lecture, *assimilate*. After taking that all in, I gathered my composure, put out my cigarette, and went back to join the rest of my friends.

By now it had been hours since the show let out, but the lobby was still a haze of stoned madness. Something was distinctly different now, though. Three cops were speaking with an irate hotel manager. The police, it seemed, were there for me. Quickly, I got out of their line of sight and picked up the house phone to call the room.

"The cops are on their way up. Hide everything," I told Jonah before going back to the car. My plan was to wait there until the police left, and then go back up to join my friends. But the cops didn't come out. Instead, it was my friends who appeared, belongings in hand. I had gotten us kicked out.

Surprisingly, no one was all that pissed, but as we pulled out of the parking lot, I remembered something urgent:

My New Year's tickets were in a drawer.

The idea of going back to a room likely still occupied by officers seemed preposterous. But this was New Year's Eve we were talking about. So, while it was definitely a foolish act, Elias agreed to go back on my behalf. As he exited the car to engage in this dangerous mission, I thought I should clue him in on one small detail:

"Oh, and there's two hits of ecstasy in the drawer."

We waited in that car for an eternity, praying that Elias would come out alone—without cops and not in handcuffs. When he eventually appeared, we exhaled and tried to figure out where we could spend the night.

* * *

A week or so after the New Year's Run, I stopped by SU's Marshall Street on my way home from OCC. The dingy but lively strip was frequented by students from all walks of life, but for the upscale Long Island and Jersey crowd, there were only three viable spots. The first was Harry's. The second was The Bagel Diner, an ode to the suburban NYC breakfast joint. And third was Le Salon, a high-end beauty parlor. That's where I found myself on a Wednesday afternoon, as a cohort of girls got their hair straightened, nails painted, and brows waxed.

As I entered, everyone looked bewildered, like, "Why is this dirty hippie in this gross yellow jacket and clunky wool hat here?" When I took my beanie off to reveal a knotty mess of half-hearted dreadlocks, that reaction turned to disgust and, finally, amusement.

"Have a seat," one of the ladies said.

It was time for a change. I was in the process of applying to SU, Johnny was locked up for at least a few years, and chopping off my natty dreads was the next logical step towards assimilation. Forty-five minutes later and with a nearly shaved head, I arrived on south campus, where my friends from The Mount now lived, right below the rock quarry. Natalie and Erin were roommates, and their place was the hangout spot.

Natalie's room was filled with fliers from raves and other Techno-related paraphernalia. That was her thing, and she wasn't alone. For the past year or so, electronica continued to permeate campus, moving from a small group of kids into the alternative mainstream. The scene was similar to that of Phish, centered around music and drug-infused dancing. We tripped; they rolled.

I wasn't into techno, but it intrigued me. So, I read a couple of related books, even heading to my old stomping grounds at Seven Rays Bookstore. The earlier days of the scene had a real purpose to it, from its DIY ethos to a soul nourishing community. But from what I could see, that had faded. Now it was more like a fashionable group of hipsters and other derelicts who just liked to get fucked up.

When it was announced that a huge rave, or *party*, would take place at a State Fairgrounds warehouse, it was the talk of the town. That hype reminded me of The Spot from freshman year, except my friends were trying to convince me to go instead of ragging on it. Cool lights, trippy music, tons of drugs, and dancing, they said. It was totally up my alley, claimed another. Truth be told, they didn't have to twist my arm that hard. If anything, I considered it part of my assimilation process. Less hippie, more techno. I agreed to go.

Two months later, I found myself in a packed and dark warehouse with glow sticks and a few bush-league lights serving as the only sources of illumination. Natalie had tried to convince me to take something to get the full experience. The way she spoke sounded like my spiel to Petta and Craig back in October. But I had sworn off psychedelics—again. Ecstasy was still an option, though, and I was on the lookout for some.

When I ran into my buddy Derek Castle, who was there with some friends, we struggled to understand each other over the loud music and thunderous bass. He handed me a small piece of paper, and I heard the word "acid" two or three times. He was definitely asking a question, but all I could make out was that he was offering me a dose.

"I can't," I said, my words getting drowned out by the immense sound system.

"What?!"

Neither of us could hear each other.

I tried pushing the dose back in Derek's hands, but he was persistent. It was not like Derek to be so pushy—he didn't do a lot of drugs. But deep down somewhere I must have wanted to trip. Maybe it was the music. Maybe it was the lights.

Maybe I just had no fucking self-control.

I took the paper from Derek and put it in my mouth— after all, it was only one dose. But Derek freaked out. He rambled nervously, but I couldn't tell what he was saying. But eventually I got it. He was telling me I didn't just take a dose.

"I wanted you to separate them for me. My hands are shaking too hard."

I had taken several.

I spat the paper into my hand. It had only been in my mouth a second or two, but I didn't know what that meant in terms of dosage. There was nothing I could do, so I hoped for the best and ventured out to dance.

Jam-band music and eletronica were worlds apart, but they shared a very important feature: the ability to transport you to a different state of consciousness. A couple hours after taking however much acid that was, the creepy voice on the Josh Wink track "Are You there?" broke that mental barrier, its rhythm penetrating deep into my skull.

Are you there? The voice crackled like it was coming through a CB radio.

Boom-boom-boom-boom-boom-boom-boom-boom.

Are you there? It seemed to be speaking directly to me now.

Yes, I'm here. I'm listening.

Boom-boom-boom-boom-boom-boom-boom-boom.

Are you there? the voice asked again, the bass pounding even louder and the high-pitched sounds growing more assertive.

Are you there, are you theeeeeeeeeere?

Yeah, man, I was *there*. I threw my hands up, surrendering to the music.

Are you there? Are you there? Are you theeeeeeeeeeere?

My body adjusted to the increasingly dense breakbeats, and as the music took control, the hemp necklace tightened around my neck. I used two fingers to stretch it out, but its grasp only grew stronger. Strobe lights illuminated Nautica and DKNY labels, glow sticks, and other elements of the techno scene. The room suddenly appeared coordinated, like the security guards towards the end of that Dave Matthews show in Binghamton. I panicked. How could I not see it? The rave scene was part of the movement. The dancing, the drugs, it connected all of us. And it was no accident that I ended up here tonight.

Are you there?

No, I'm not. I've lost it. I continued to struggle with the necklace, but it wasn't coming off; and as I stood there, choking, the room froze. I felt the, "We interrupt your regularly scheduled programming" graphic coalescing. Like Chicago, I had been lured here. I fell for the hype of the event. The *rave* of it all. And I wanted no part of it.

Are you there?

Boom-boom-boom-boom-boom-boom-boom-boom.

Where's my jacket?

Are you there?

Fuck it, I don't need my jacket.

Are you there?

I ran for the exit.

Are you theeeeeeeeeeere?

I exited the warehouse, gasping for air, but eventually got a grip. I was walking away when I heard voices calling my name. It was three girls who were now seniors at Nottingham, Laura, Jen, and Nicole. They noticed something was off with me and were concerned. My friend Derek came outside and explained about the doses. The girls offered to take me to Denny's with them, but first I needed to get that damn jacket. So, while they stood outside smoking clove cigarettes, Derek offered to take me into the warehouse to find it.

"I can't go back in there, dude. There's no way."

"It's fine, man. I'll walk with you. I'd go myself, but I don't know what your jacket looks like."

I was like a three-year-old whose father was trying to get him to enter a haunted house at a Halloween carnival.

"Fine," I said, "but hold my hand."

* * *

As I entered the warehouse, I was terrified. The only thing keeping me settled was Derek's hand. We searched each room for my jacket. When we entered the jungle music area, I saw a bone-skinny dude with strung-out eyes. It was Jake McCallistair. He was in bad shape.

Once we found my coat, I ran back to the girls outside. We went to Denny's, blasting tunes while driving down Erie Boulevard. I was still a bit shaken up, but beginning to feel much more like myself, when a new song came on Laura's CD mix. It began with a few seconds of dramatic, almost spooky sounding, solo piano. The arpeggiated minor notes were familiar, but I was unable to place them. The quick movement of the pianist's fingers seemed to dance along my shivering spine. Suddenly, it was like a filter was pulled over my eyes—the bright lights of a stage going down. I was on the set of *This is Your Life*. I had no choice but to give in and listen.

I remembered the song. It was a favorite during those disco nights at Style High. But now it wasn't about a love-torn woman having the guts to kick out her abusive lover. It was about my relationship with LSD.

At first I was afraid, I was petrified,
kept thinking I could never live without you by my side.

I learned in Binghamton that my hallucinations were what I needed to transform into a better version of me. But there was nothing left for me to learn from psychedelics, and so much I could lose. I was done.

But then I spent so many nights thinking how you did me wrong,
and I grew strong,
and I learned how to get along ...

"This is my shit." I asked the girls to turn it up as the dramatic opening segued into a frenetic disco beat.

And so you're back
from outer space.
I just walked in to find you here with that sad look upon your face,
I should have changed that stupid lock, I should have made you leave your key,
if I'd known for just one second you'd be back to bother me ...

"Yes!"

Go on now, go,

WALK OUT THE DOOR,
just turn around now,
'cause you're not welcome anymore …

I stuck my head out the window, and while we cruised down the street and pulled into the Denny's parking lot, I sang on the top of my lungs:

Oh no, not I,
I will survive,
oh, as long as I know how to love, I know I'll stay alive,
I've got all my life to live,
and I've got all my love to give and I'll survive.

By the time we left Denny's, I was exhausted. I had spent our time at the diner apologizing to my glass of water because I hadn't been drinking enough of it lately. When I got dropped off at home, I said my goodbyes and walked to my porch. But I quickly stopped in my tracks when I saw a huge, oversized envelope stuffed into my mailbox. Back in high school, people said that if a college denied you, you got a regular mail-sized envelope, but if you got in—big envelope. Well, this thing was huge.

As I walked into my house, I excitedly ripped it open, and there, right on the cover letter, were the words, "Congratulations on your acceptance to Syracuse University!" I couldn't believe it. I still had to get into Newhouse, but this was an enormous step forward. And as I triumphantly walked up to my attic bedroom, I imagined those magnificent string instruments and irresistible beat.

I will survive! Hey hey!

I LEARNED IT BY WATCHING YOU

As I walked into Syracuse University's Gifford Auditorium on a warm evening in 1983, I imagined the tortuous things taught there. Chalk dust permeated throughout the lecture hall and made me feel like I was in school, not out for a fun Saturday night with my big brother Jeff. And as everyone congregated in the lobby waiting for the main event—a big screen marathon of *The Three Stooges*—beers were poured from a keg. Within minutes, I was impressing Jeff's friends with my Curley impressions, garnering a slew of laughs and high fives. I was a six-year-old kid up way past his bedtime, and I was killing it.

Thirteen years later in the very same lecture hall, it wasn't Larry, Curly, and Moe I was listening to, but an anthropology professor's diatribe on Australopithecus Afarensis. It was now 1999. After two years of busting my ass at SU, I had earned my acceptance into the Newhouse school. It was late afternoon on a Thursday, and with no classes on Fridays, it was time to go home and relax before hitting the bars.

On my way out, I grabbed a *Daily Orange*, the school paper. I was stunned to read about a local drug bust. Ziggy—the late-night food truck guy that I hit with a rock years ago—had been dealing blow. His wagon, it turned out, was also a cokemobile. I thought of the irony as I walked home, paper in hand like a commemorative program from a football game.

That night, I went to Marshall Street. It hadn't changed much. Harry's was still there and served the same clientele, but two things were markedly different than the night that Shai—who was now doing well at OCC and about to transfer to SUNY Binghamton—got blackballed. The first was that Zopie's had closed and Harry's had expanded into that space. The second was that I was actually in line to get in, dressed in a button-down Banana Republic shirt, with gel in my hair, surrounded by a cloud of Calvin Klein's Eternity cologne.

I met up with Petta and walked down a set of stairs into what was once my old coffee shop. Eight identically dressed girls sat on top of the bar, swaying to some rap song that I didn't know—although I recognized the *Little Orphan Annie* tune it sampled.

The girls, in their skin-tight black capri pants, diamond jewelry, and straightened hair, had their hands in the air, singing along to every word. They were the least qualified people imaginable to relate to the "hard knock life" the artist was rapping about.

Moments later, I greeted some chicks I knew with kisses on the cheek and fist bumped some guy friends, their blingy Movados and Tag Heuers reflecting light into my face. I grabbed a Jack & Coke and scanned the room. I recognized some faces from The Mount—not people I'd ever spoken to, but the ones I saw in the lobby from my dad's van before that night at the quarry. I thought about how much had changed in three years, and now I was *here* with *them*. I had engaged in a deliberate effort to assimilate, but once that decision had been made, everything else was subconscious.

It was nearing last call when Petta, a few others, and I snagged a booth by the front window, a coveted spot where one could watch the action outside. Someone brought up the name Samantha. The rumor was that she had been buying coke from Ziggy for months, and after being nabbed during a surveillance operation, she became an informant. It was her, they said, who got Ziggy busted. She had left campus and wasn't coming back.

I glanced outside and saw familiar faces looking in. It was Jason and Jared, the cool kids from my childhood. The ones who tossed the lingerie model on my desk and who whispered under their breath moments before I was asked to leave high school. I tried to get their attention, but they couldn't see me. They were on something and looked different. Their clean-cut veneers had overgrown into long hair, unkempt faces, and bleak futures. The look in their dilated eyes told me exactly what they were thinking. I knew how this terrible scene and its obnoxious people looked to a couple of townies.

* * *

Abe was still awake when I stumbled home at two. It was not a huge surprise to see him in the dining room, but I couldn't fathom why he'd still be waiting up for me. Back in the day, when there was a good chance he'd get a call from the cops or a hospital, the anxiety made sense. But there was no longer much to worry about. I got into SU. Not just SU, but Newhouse. I earned a merit-based scholarship and was on the dean's list. Why was he sitting in the dark worrying? Why couldn't he just close his door and go to bed?

It wasn't easy to get my dad to talk. But after a long hesitation, he recounted the long trip to, and from, Siberia. He spoke of being trapped in a train car with several other families for days, with no idea of where they were going or when they would get there. There was the suffering, the hunger, and the inhumane conditions. It was because of that experience that he couldn't sleep in an enclosed room. That's why once Cholo and I inadvertently woke him up, there would be no going back to sleep. He was haunted.

He didn't say any of that exactly—he would never allow himself to be vulnerable—but he didn't need to. As Cholo came over to nudge me to bed, the heaviness of generational trauma hung in the air.

"Why didn't you just say that years ago?" I asked lightheartedly and walked up the stairs with Cholo right behind me.

ANY QUESTIONS?

The Arclight Cinema in West Hollywood, California was lit up for two related occasions—the holiday shopping season and the premiere of the movie *Elf*. And while the Christmas decorations looked no different from the ones I'd grown up around, the fact that it was nearly eighty degrees made it a galaxy away from Syracuse. I said hi to Will Farrell as I walked to my reserved seat for the screening.

In 2000, I graduated and went to work in feature film development for MTV Films. While I had long ago understood that my mission to change the world was a hallucination, in the back of my head, I couldn't help but appreciate that I was working my way up in Viacom, just as I thought I was commanded to do. But I had left MTV for New Line eighteen months prior, working on the development and production of what would become a holiday classic. My biggest contribution to the film was writing the bit where Will Farrell gives James Caan lingerie he spotted at a department store. It was inspired by the Sears rip-out Robbie Cornbloom brought to class that day in first grade.

After six years in the film business, I moved to Manhattan to get my MBA from New York University's Stern School of Business, where I referred to New Yorkers who didn't attend NYU as townies.

My rationalization for the MBA was that the business experience would complement my creative background, and that after two years I'd head back to LA. A summer position at Google's Mountain View headquarters was promising, and it allowed me to catch up with Darren, who had become a mortgage broker in San Francisco. But life had other plans. Two months before graduation, I met my fiancé, Sandy, and was set to get married on, coincidentally, Halloween of 2010. Shai, who had attended law school and worked in celebrity media and my brother Jeff were my best men. My first dance with Sandy would be to "*Thriller*".

While the delusions of that experience had long subsided, I thought of it often, especially when I would read how psychedelic therapy was entering the mainstream. I mean, I didn't need to be convinced. I attributed my success in life to psychedelic experiences, and I likely would have been in jail, or worse, without them. But I couldn't see how such things would play out in a clinical setting. How would a therapist react to my getting naked in her office?

It was weird living in the city. The Peep World in which I once ran amok was now a Hooters. The Hotel Pennsylvania was still there, and every year when Phish played the Garden during the holidays, I'd take a stroll through the lobby and reminisce about my old stomping grounds. But now I was at Bergdorf

A DOSE OF REALITY

Goodman with Sandy, picking out a bowtie for my wedding, when Stapes texted me a YouTube link. While he dropped out of SU sophomore year, he and I still spoke. The last time we connected I'd asked him to be a groomsman, to which his response was, "You were shackled on Halloween fifteen years ago, now you want to do it all over again?"

I clicked on Stape's link, which took me to the Fourth of July show Phish had just played in Atlanta. They played "Harpua"—that song whose narration about Jimmy sent me over the edge in Chicago and forever changed my life. I listened to Trey's narration and got why Stapes had sent it to me.

"I'm sure that most of you know that the history they teach you in school books is a little inaccurate. This is such a beautiful country, but I hate to break it to you: Most of the things you've read are lies. The thing I'm trying to tell you here tonight is that isn't okay, and that interlaced within the lyrics of every Phish song is the actual history of this amazing country. You have to be very accurate and look at all the lyrics as a whole. We've spent thousands of hours crafting these songs, and it's like a mystery you have to glue together."

I glanced over at Sandy. I had finally met my Jill Campbell. But, she didn't know how borderline insane I'd once been, and who knew how she'd react to that? Back on the phone, Trey continued his story about Jimmy. Just like in Chicago, he was sitting in his apartment listening to one of his all-time favorite bands.

"It happened to be one of the only bands other than Phish who won't bullshit you and who will tell you the truth in their songs. And

Jimmy's really cranking it up and rocking out. And it sounds something like this."

Then Phish let out four super loud, suspenseful, and distorted chords followed by an all too familiar bass line. I knew this song, but it took the following six percussive accentuations for me to place it. And as the band proceeded to cover this fantastically aggressive song, I thought, *Holy fucking shit.*

It was "Killing in the Name," by Rage Against the Machine.

I put down the phone and stood for a moment, thinking about a much different time, when my life was in an extraordinarily different place.

"What is it?" Sandy said, causing me to snap back to reality. It took a moment, but I was able to collect my composure.

"Just a concert."

In Memory of
Abraham Silverbush

www.ingramcontent.com/pod-product-compliance
Lightning Source LLC
Chambersburg PA
CBHW020245010526
44107CB00002B/106